Praise for *The Kid's Guide to Social Action*

"A tremendously useful, well-organized, and inspiring book!"

—Children's Television Workshop

"If you've been wondering about how to prepare future leaders of our nation, here's a place to start."

—*School Library Journal*

"A wealth of information for kids who want to change things."

—*ALA Booklist*

"A great handbook that paves the way for successful, meaningful community projects orchestrated by kids."

—*Chicago Sun-Times* (Book Week)

"The liveliest practical civics book for young students in print."

—Ralph Nader

Awards received by *The Kid's Guide to Social Action*

"Best of the Best for Children"

—American Library Association

"Books for the Teen Age Selection"

—New York Public Library

"Outstanding Children's Book, Reading-Magic Awards"

—*Parenting Magazine*

"Children's Book of Distinction Award"

—*Hungry Mind Review*

As Seen On

CBS "This Morning"
CBS "Raising Good Kids in Bad Times"
CNN "Newsroom"
CNN "Headline News"

THE KID'S GUIDE TO SOCIAL ACTION

How to solve the social problems *you choose*— and turn creative thinking into positive action

Barbara A. Lewis

Edited by Pamela Espeland

free Spirit®

PUBLISHING

Library of Congress Cataloging-in-Publication Data
Lewis, Barbara A., 1943–
     The kid's guide to social action: how to solve the social problems you choose—and turn creative thinking into positive action/Barbara A. Lewis
     p.   cm.
     Includes bibliographical references and index.
     Summary: Resource guide for children for learning political action skills that can help them make a difference in solving social problems at the community, state, and national levels.
     ISBN: 0-915793-29-6: $14.95
     1. Social problems—Handbooks, manuals, etc.—Juvenile literature. 2. Social action—United States—Handbooks, manuals, etc.—Juvenile literature. 3. Political participation—United States—Handbooks, manuals, etc.—Juvenile literature. 4. Problem solving—Handbooks, manuals, etc.—Juvenile literature. [1. Social action. 2. Political participation. 3. Politics, Practical] I. Title.
HN65.L442   1991
361.2—dc20   90-44297
                                                  CIP
                                                  AC

Printed in the United States of America
10 9 8

Cover and text design by MacLean & Tuminelly
Cover Illustration by Lisa Wagner
Cover Photography by Paul Lundquist
Illustrations by Steve Michaels

FREE SPIRIT PUBLISHING INC.
400 First Avenue North, Suite 616
Minneapolis, MN 55401
(612) 338-2068

"Kids in Action: Jackson Elementary" is based on an article by the author which originally appeared in *Sierra Magazine*, March/April 1989. "Ten Steps for Taking Social Action" originally appeared in *Free Spirit: News & Views on Growing Up*, Vol. 3, No. 4, March/April 1990. Ideas for the brainstorming forms on pages 14, 15, 153, and 154 were inspired by the Talents Unlimited Model, Mobile County School System, and the Future Problem Solving Model, Laurinburg, North Carolina. Much information on the worldwide activities of youth was contributed by the United Nations Environment Program (UNEP), to which we are grateful. The letter to the editor on page 28 is courtesy Hal Knight, *Deseret News*. The survey forms on pages 46, 159, 160, and 161 are adapted with permission from "Bill of Rights Newsletter," 8, number 2, page 4, Constitutional Rights Foundation, Los Angeles, California, 1974. Much information on grants is based on *A Citizen's Guide to Community Education*, The League of Women Voters Education Fund, Washington, D.C., 1988, pages 35-53. "Kids in Action: Audrey Chase" is courtesy Dave Block, KLS-TV News, Salt Lake City. Information about Youth Force is from the National Crime Prevention Council, Washington, D.C.; the story is used with permission of the Citizens Committee for New York City, Inc. Much information on state governments, including the State House Contacts chart on pages 129–130, is from *The Book of States*, The Council of State Governments, Lexington, Kentucky, 1988-1989, with 1990 updates, and is used with their permission. Much information on resolutions is from "How to Write a Resolution," page 3, from *Study Guide for "How To,"* courtesy the Utah Association of Women Executive Board, Salt Lake City, Utah, 1985. The photo of the KAP kids on page 123 is courtesy *U.S. News & World Report*.

To kids everywhere.
May you be both *seen* and *heard*.

CONTENTS

CONTENTS

CONTENTS

CONTENTS

CONTENTS

ACKNOWLEDGMENTS

Special thanks to my publisher, Judy Galbraith, for believing in me, and in the abilities of kids to create social action.

Thanks to my editor, Pamela Espeland, for patience, encouragement, cheerfulness, and fine editing skills.

A special recognition to Olene Walker, the Salt Lake Education Foundation, and Chevron USA, Inc. for their support of my initial grant in Community Problem Solving, and to Project 2000 Kidspeak for encouragement.

I have gleaned much information and instruction on teaching critical thinking skills from many individuals, a few of whom I would like to recognize as having especially influenced my thinking:

▶ Anne Crabbe, Director of the International Future Problem Solving Program, for inspiration and for her dedication in teaching children and adults how to solve community problems;

▶ Sydney Parnes and Alex Osbourne, for the original Creative Problem Solving Model, which combined critical thinking with action in an understandable way;

▶ Calvin Taylor and the Talents Unlimited staff in the Mobile County Public School System, for their marvelous program for teaching kids to think creatively;

▶ Joseph Renzulli, for his Triad Model; Barbara Clark, for opening new vistas of what the brain can do; Sandra Kaplan, for her thematic approach to teaching and differentiated curriculum.

Hats off to all the children and their parents in the Extended Learning Program at Jackson Elementary, and to all the other kids and their advisers who have contributed stories to this book.

For believing in young folks, a special thank you to all the community groups, educators, legislators, administrators, and officials who have supported the Jackson children in their projects; and to my principal, Pete Gallegos, and Salt Lake School District for the courage to allow freedom and flexibility in my program.

And lastly, a special kiss to my husband, Larry, and children, Mike, Andrea, Chris, and Sam, for their patience, inspiration, and continued love.

INTRODUCTION

Have you ever been sprawled on the carpet, munching chips, while watching a TV reporter discuss a problem in the news? You may have said to yourself, "I know what I'd do if I were in charge." You saw the solution clearly—somewhere between the time when you dipped a chip in the salsa and crunched it between your teeth. And yet, you wondered, who would listen to you?

You might be shocked at the number of people who would not only listen to you, but also act on your suggestions. Kids around the world are tackling mountains of community problems. And adults are standing with hands on hips and gaping mouths as they witness kids pushing through laws, cleaning up vacant lots, collecting a billion tons of newspapers to recycle, even making pets out of endangered protozoa. These aren't superkids with magical powers. They're regular kids, just like you.

The Kid's Guide to Social Action can help you transform your creative thinking into actions that make a difference in your neighborhood, your town or city, your state, your country, and your world. And it's written for kids so even adults can understand and use it. But this isn't a book of lesson plans. It isn't a book of ready-made projects. It won't tell you what to do. It *will* give you the skills you need to solve the social problems you choose.

How to Read This Book

You can dip your toes and wade through different sections, or you can dive in and swim from cover to cover. It's up to you. But it may help to know that this book is divided into five main parts.

▶ PART ONE: LIFE BEYOND THE CLASSROOM

Meet the kids from Jackson Elementary School in Salt Lake City, Utah, whose efforts resulted in the cleanup of a hazardous waste site, the passage of two new laws, the planting of hundreds of trees, and sidewalk improvements. Learn how you, too, can create projects that make a difference.

▶ PART TWO: POWER SKILLS

Master the social action skills you need to accomplish your projects. Learn how to write letters, create surveys, pass petitions, picket—even get TV coverage and raise big bucks. You'll see samples of student work and pictures of kids in action.

▶ PART THREE: INITIATING OR CHANGING LAWS

Grown-ups aren't the only ones who can make or change laws. Kids are doing it, too. Read about a group of gutsy kids from New Jersey who are going for a Constitutional Amendment. Learn how to lobby—how to convince your legislators to vote for *your* bill.

▶ PART FOUR: RESOURCES

This part points you toward more information—important phone numbers and addresses, groups you may want to join, places to apply for awards, and more. Learn who to call, where to write, and how to get the recognition you deserve.

▶ PART FIVE: TOOLS

Petitions, proclamations, releases, and resolutions—these are just some of the tools of social action. In this part, you'll find the forms you need to put your best foot forward. They're ready for you to photocopy and use.

Throughout *The Kid's Guide to Social Action*, you'll read about other action "bench pressers" who have accomplished everything from saving a courthouse to feeding the homeless. You'll meet Alison Stieglitz, who adopted a shelter for abused and abandoned teenagers. And high school students Rikki Ashley and Rob Osborne, who worked to get a slab of cement for kids to "cruise" around. And the "Tree Musketeers," pint-sized Johnny Appleseeds. You'll even learn of a young African from Zambia who operates a barefoot troupe of actors.

All of these kids are heroes. But they're also ordinary kids who just want to design a better future.

If you have a social action story you'd like to share about yourself or someone you know, write it down and send it to:

> Barbara Lewis
> c/o Free Spirit Publishing Inc.
> 400 First Avenue North, Suite 616
> Minneapolis, MN 55401

If possible, include a telephone number where you can be reached. Your story may be used in future books or articles.

Solving social problems will bring excitement and suspense into your life. Instead of reading dusty textbooks and memorizing what other people have done, you'll create your own history with the actions you take. And here's a promise to you: As you reach out to solve problems in your community, you'll be helping to design a better future. You'll also be learning to take charge of your personal life. You'll become more confident in yourself, because you'll prove to yourself that you can do almost anything.

> **❝ Parents can only give good advice or put [their children] on the right paths, but the final forming of a person's character lies in their own hands. ❞**
>
> *Anne Frank,*
> The Diary of a Young Girl

Social Action: What's In It for You?

Social action includes those things you do that extend beyond your own home and classroom into the "real world." These things aren't required of you. You don't *have* to do them. You do them selflessly, to improve the quality of life around you.

The real world is chock-full of real problems to solve: real letters to write, real laws waiting to be made, real surveys to analyze, real streams needing monitoring, scraggly landscapes in need of artistic attention.

Isn't it exciting for you that all these problems haven't already been solved? Could you think of anything more boring than growing up in a world where everything had already been done, and there was nothing left for you to do?

Why Should You Care?

This is the Age of the Kid. The world needs to see your work and to hear your voice. And *you* need to start asserting and enjoying your rights.

Think about it. There have been many social movements to define and strengthen adults' rights. For example, you've probably read about the women's rights movement. Before it got started and grew strong, many people thought that women weren't smart enough or interested enough to take social action, do certain kinds of jobs, even vote in elections. The minorities' rights movements are working to increase opportunities for people who have long been discriminated against. There's even an animals' rights movement underway.

But what about *kids'* rights? For years, kids were told to be "seen and not heard." That's not so true anymore. Or is it? Are kids represented on neighborhood committees or school boards where you live? Do your senators ask your opinions before making or changing laws?

Do you find it insulting that most adults think you're only interested in video games and loud music? Are you tired of adults making most of the big decisions that affect your life? Kids are probably the most *un*represented group in the world. Now, some adults might disagree and say that your parents represent you. But there was a time when women heard that their husbands represented them. What's the difference?

No one can represent you better than you. You have a fresh view of life. You don't know all the reasons why something *won't* work. You're willing to try new things. You come up with new ideas. And you have your own opinions.

But your opinions won't be presented to the public unless *you* get out there and do it. Of course, you'll still want to schedule a few video games in between, and take time for music and other things you like to do. When you start working for social change, you don't stop having fun.

Maybe you're not interested in solving *big* problems. That's okay. There are many ways to make a difference, and *The Kid's Guide* will introduce you to quite a few. If you're one of those kids who wants to change the world, this book is for you. Or if you're just one of those kids who gets the uncontrollable urge to stand up in a movie theater and shout, "I'll rip the arms off the next person who throws an empty popcorn cup or sticky wad of gum on the floor!"—this book is for you, too.

Barbara A. Lewis

> **❝ One of the virtues of being very young is that you don't let the facts get in the way of your imagination. ❞**
>
> *Sam Levenson*

CREATE YOUR OWN FUTURE

WHEREAS,   You are capable of thinking and solving real problems, you should not allow adults (or anyone else) to put you down. Don't pay attention to those who say you can't succeed if you're poor, uneducated, or disabled, or because you're a minority, a girl, or a child. Don't get trapped by those chilling excuses. They can make you numb. You *can* succeed.

WHEREAS,   You can make a difference in the world, don't listen to those who insist it's too late to breathe fresh air, control neighborhood gangs, save the rain forests, save the whales, combat drug abuse, and create world peace. It's only too late when *you* stop believing in the future.

WHEREAS,   You can find your own problems and design your own solutions, be suspicious of anyone who "gives" you a problem to solve or wants you to resolve a pet project. Decide what *you* want to work on, then invite others to join *your* team.

WHEREAS,   You should *not* feel responsible for solving all the world's problems while you're still a kid, neither should you feel excluded from creating solutions. Don't be swayed by people who say you're "too young," that you should spend these years dreaming and just being a kid. Remind them of how it feels to be powerless. They will remember. The ability to solve problems doesn't belong just to adults—and the ability to dream doesn't belong just to kids.

WHEREAS,   You have the right to shape your future, don't wait for someone else to do it for you. Speak up. Speak out. Design a world you want to live in. Don't wait for luck to create it. Luck is just another word for work. The world needs to see your works and to hear your voices.

NOW, THEREFORE,   Be it resolved that the Decade of the Nineties shall be proclaimed as:

THE KID'S DECADE FOR SOCIAL ACTION

for all kids who believe in themselves, each other, and the future. Don't *allow* life to happen. *Make* it happen!

SIGNED AND SEALED this 1st day of February, 1991.

Barbara A. Lewis

BARBARA A. LEWIS, Teacher

LIFE
BEYOND
THE
CLASSROOM

PART ONE

Jackson Elementary

Salt Lake City, Utah. Black dots representing possible hazardous waste sites were sprinkled across the large wall map of Salt Lake City like flecks of pepper. I had hung the eight-foot map on the blackboard so my students could see it easily. They discovered that one of the sites was located just three blocks from our school.

"That old barrel yard?" 11-year-old Maxine asked, shocked at how close the site was to us. "Kids climb all over those barrels!"

"I bet there are at least a thousand barrels in one pile," added Chris. He grabbed a marking pen and circled the spot.

We were studying the importance of groundwater, the underground liquid cities pump up for people to drink. We had learned that hazardous waste can leak down to contaminate the water. I had planned the unit for my academically talented sixth graders at Jackson Elementary, where I teach special classes of fourth through sixth graders. I had no idea I was unleashing a tiger. Wait until you hear what these kids did.

As it turned out, Chris had underestimated: The site held 50,000 barrels that at one time had contained everything from molasses and flour to dangerous chemicals. Now, after a recycling business had stockpiled them for more than 40 years, many were rusted and corroded. Residues left in the barrels had long since dribbled out onto the bare dirt.

"Who could we ask to find out whether our water supply has been contaminated?" I asked the kids.

"The health department," Heather suggested. She always grabbed the attention of the other kids, despite her tiny size and soft voice.

As the sixth graders' enthusiasm grew, the fourth and fifth graders jumped on the bandwagon. We now had 34

kids tackling the problem. This was as exciting to them as unraveling a mystery, since it was *their* neighborhood.

I made preliminary phone calls to alert officials that students would be calling to ask what they might do to help. "There's nothing children can do," one health department official told me. "They'll be in high school before they see any results."

Later, when the kids themselves called the officials, they were shooed away like pesky flies. But since I teach the children to solve problems, they didn't give up. They just looked for new solutions.

The next idea was to conduct a door-to-door survey of their industrial neighborhood, informing residents about the dangers of hazardous waste and searching for wells. Why wells? The kids thought they could ask health officials to take water samples.

These two strategies didn't work, either. In a four-block area that included several abandoned houses and warehouses with wooden planks slapped haphazardly over jagged window glass, the children discovered only a few wells, all cemented over. But what surprised them more was the "I-don't-care" response from the locals.

Before returning to school, we paused outside the barrel site fence. Covering three blocks, the steel mountain of drums blocked the children's view of a community sports arena, the Mormon Temple, and the Wasatch Mountains in the distance.

"Look," Maxine said, pointing. "Some of the barrels are orange and yucky."

"Rusted," Chris said.

"And some have big holes."

"Corroded," Chris corrected.

"Look at all the orange colors in the dirt," Heather said, "and black, too. I wonder if anything leaked out of the barrels."

Maxine bent down. "The fence has lots of holes in it," she said. "Bet I could climb through one."

The "protective" fence sagged in spots like stretched-out potbellies. In a later survey of the school's students, 32 children would admit to having played on the barrels.

"I've seen bums build fires in those barrels," one kid said now.

"Chemicals in the bottoms could cause an explosion," another added.

Kory's brown eyes popped. "And blow up the whole school!"

"Don't exaggerate," Chris scoffed.

But Kory wasn't that far off. We had read of an explosion in Elizabeth, New Jersey, where only 10,000 barrels had been stockpiled. The site had exploded and created a toxic cloud extending for a quarter of a mile in every direction. When firefighters put out the fire, the runoff spilled into the Elizabeth River and polluted it.

So the children listened to Chris, but not really.

While we were at the site, some of the kids decided to stop at the barrel yard's office. A worker who answered the children's knock told the kids to bug off, that there weren't any problems at the site.

A newspaper reporter had tagged along after the kids to cover their story. He questioned the man, too. The worker argued that no chemicals from the drums had ever leaked onto the dirt, and that the owner had never accepted barrels that had more than an inch of residue in the bottoms. Growing red-faced, the worker insisted that they had spent more than $50,000 in the past few years to meet regulations set by the Environmental Protection Agency (EPA).

But my kids weren't convinced. "What happened to the ground before we had those laws?" Heather asked when we were back in the classroom.

To learn more, they began reading articles on hazardous waste in such magazines as the *New England Journal of Medicine*, *Newsweek*, and *U.S. News & World Report*. Sound like hard reading? You're right. But the kids devoured the articles, because it was *their* problem. They learned that hazardous waste could cause brain damage, nerve problems, even cancer.

I went to the health department and got copies of dozens of articles that had been published in local newspapers over the past six months. The kids read them all. It was the first time the newspapers had been really interesting to them.

An environmental consultant, health officials, and Salt Lake City's emergency hazardous waste cleanup team came to our class to lecture. Health officials told us that even one inch of dangerous chemicals could leak down through the soil and contaminate groundwater.

With all the information they now had, the kids felt like junior experts. They brainstormed new solutions to the problem.

Shauna called the EPA's national hotline to ask for help. Other students wrote to the agency's regional office in Denver. Another called the local power company, which owned the land where the barrels were stockpiled.

TV and radio stations and newspapers covered the stories.

But things didn't start changing until the students visited Salt Lake City Mayor Palmer DePaulis. Lucky for the kids, he had been a schoolteacher. He listened to them. Then he amazed them. He promised to work toward getting the mess cleaned up within 18 months! The kids struggled to walk instead of run out the door.

Jackson kids at the barrel site, where 50,000 barrels had stockpiled over 40 years. Some had contained residues of hazardous waste.

Courtesy Paul Barker, *Deseret News*

Once outside, they slapped "high fives" into each others' hands and showed off with a few flips and cartwheels on the front lawn.

Within a few weeks, changes began at the barrel site. Under all the public pressure from people the children had contacted, and the coverage in the media, workers started removing the barrels.

In early June 1987 just a few months after the kids had begun their campaign, researchers from the Denver EPA office came to Utah to check out the site. Although the sixth graders were enjoying their graduation party, many chose to leave the party and scramble over to the barrel site to watch the EPA dig their own wells to check the water. They came in dresses and pressed pants, straight from the dance. (Like you, they usually prefer torn jeans and stretched-out tees. And like you, they usually prefer parties to pollution inspection.)

The girls twirled around, catching the breeze in puffed-out skirts, then arm-wrestled with the boys. Heather won.

"We did it!" they shouted. "Kids *can* make a difference!"

Results of the test were promised within nine months.

But the kids' pride faded when they learned that the owner of the barrel yard had suffered a heart attack and was in intensive care at a hospital. To make it worse, one of his workers said that the pollution dispute had probably helped to cause his heart attack. "Don't you know that this man has contributed thousands of dollars to the local children's hospital, Little League teams, and other charities?" the man scolded. "We're not contaminating anything. By recycling, we're cleaning up the environment."

If you're confused, so were the kids. They learned that things are seldom all right or all wrong. They thought about this through summer recess. They leaned on the fence by the barrel yard and watched the removal of the barrels by truck and train. The piles shrank. Bare patches appeared on the dirt. Within a year, all the drums would disappear, leaving only the stained soil behind.

In the meantime, I received three anonymous phone calls threatening legal action if the kids persisted on the project. The caller was not the barrel yard owner, but another man in industry who told me we might be sued. Nothing ever came of the threats, but the school district promised free legal help if we needed it.

When the kids returned to school in the fall, I expected them to have given up their hazardous waste crusade. After all, how interesting can "garbage" be? I was wrong. Even the old sixth graders (now mature seventh graders) returned to brainstorm new strategies with the younger children. They argued over which kids would do what. They were still interested and involved.

I covered the blackboard with their storm of ideas. They wanted us to write more letters, make more phone calls and speeches, do more research.

Some of the kids were still concerned about the barrel yard owner. Was it really their fault that he was in the hospital? Did winning always mean that someone else had to lose?

I called the barrel yard and learned that the owner was in stable condition.

"Who besides you has rights that need to be protected?" I asked my students.

"The barrel yard owner," Chris said. "What's going to happen to small business owners like him who can't afford to clean up their messes? They could lose their businesses, and then only the big guys would be around."

Heather jumped up. "But we have a right to know what's in that dirt. We're living by it."

The other children agreed with Heather.

"Then who should be responsible for cleaning up hazardous waste?" I asked.

"Maybe the health department," one child said.

But an official spokesperson for the department had already told us that their agency didn't have any money.

"Let's earn some money to help everyone, like small businesses and people like us," one child suggested.

"And give it to the health department," another added.

"Let's clean up all the hazardous waste in the state!" Kory suggested, swinging his arms and knocking a stack of magazines to the floor.

"Get real," Chris sneered. "That would cost too much."

But they didn't give up the money idea. They held a white elephant sale and sold all their old mini-cars, doll furniture, and games with missing pieces. They raised $468.22—probably about enough to clean up one square foot of toxic mess.

Heather, always the philosopher, remained optimistic. "It's okay," she said. "It's a start."

By Christmas, the long awaited EPA test results came

Jackson kids survey the neighborhood surrounding the barrel site.

Courtesy Paul Barker, *Deseret News*

in. Heather tore down the hall, waving a large manila envelope. "The health department just brought this to the office and asked for me!" Her cheeks glowed.

We flipped through the pages together. The report indicated that harmful chemicals, solvents, coal tars, pesticides, and heavy metals had polluted the soil and groundwater at the barrel site. It listed such substances as benzene, toluene, lead, zinc, and copper. Translated, that meant that both groundwater and soil were polluted.

We didn't know it then, but the site would soon be recommended for the Utah National Priorities List. This meant that it would be given top priority for cleanup. Why? Because in the Salt Lake Valley, drinking water is collected and mixed. Our neighborhood toxic waste site threatened over 477,000 people!

Although the kids had won that battle, they didn't stop there. They mailed out 550 letters to businesses and environmental groups, asking for donations for hazardous waste cleanup. Including the money they chipped in themselves, the students raised about $2,700. They wanted to give it to the health department to help clean up any site.

But they couldn't. The law wouldn't let them.

"Let's just change the law then!" Kory said, punching his fist in the air.

The kids had read about the national Superfund, which helps clean up abandoned toxic waste sites. Utah had no such fund and ranked near the bottom of all the

states in environmental programs. So the students worked together to write up a resolution proposing a Utah State Superfund. Then the legislature turned the resolution into a bill. (A *bill* is a draft of a proposed law or change in the law.) It was called House Bill 199.

Kids lobbied legislators to vote for House Bill 199. (When you *lobby* legislators, you try to convince them to vote the way you want them to.) They called the legislators on the phone. They testified before a committee, and they even spoke to the Utah Senate when it was in session. They passed out flyers to all the legislators, trimmed in red crayon.

On the day of the vote, the kids sat on plush couches at the State House, trying to look grown-up and proper. They crossed their legs and folded their hands— but within two minutes, they were bouncing on their cushions. Then they rushed to the window. In the distance, they could see the barrel site where it had all begun almost a year before.

The lawmakers passed the bill without one vote against it. Because they weren't allowed to clap in this formal setting, the children grinned, mouths open in silent cheers, arms waving wildly.

"No one has more effectively lobbied us than these young kids," one senator said. "And they didn't even have to buy us dinner."

"These children did something we couldn't do because Superfund is such a political issue," said Brent

Bradford, a director in the health department. "They've raised the level of awareness of the whole valley to hazardous waste issues."

Since then, the kids have been invited to speak at universities, education seminars, and community groups all over Salt Lake Valley. Besides being featured in many national magazines and newspapers, they have also received at least 20 awards of appreciation, including several national awards. One of the kids' dads built a trophy case for the front hall of Jackson Elementary to show off their awards.

A local songwriter, Rosanne Markham, dedicated a song to them, "The Children, Our Future." Some of the Jackson kids were chosen to sing on the professional recording. It has become the national theme song for the Future Problem Solving Program. (If you'd like a tape, look for their address in Part Four: Resources, page 146.)

But that wasn't the end of the Jackson kids' story. When the original kids went on to junior high, new children came up with projects of their own. They graduated from garbage to sidewalks and trees. Another project brought $10,000 worth of sidewalk repairs into their neighborhood, and the kids have campaigned for more neighborhood improvements.

Like many other kids' groups across the nation, the Jackson kids turned their focus to trees. They learned from the University of Michigan's *Forestry Update* that a single tree, in its average 50-year lifetime, will contribute $62,000 worth of air pollution control. Dubbing themselves "Leaf It To Us," the younger kids decided to think big and applied for two city grants—money to use for their project. They got the grants, which totaled $3,600, and matched that with $720 they collected on their own. They adopted a park with the money and planted 107 trees there, and another 80 trees in their yards and near the school.

One day a fifth grader got a heavy idea. "Why don't we find money and make our own grants for kids all over the state to plant trees?" The Jackson kids contacted the governor, the state forester, and national forestry people. With the help of Dick Klason, State Forester, they found some national money for grants for children in Utah.

Not to be outdone by previous Jackson hotshots, the new kids tackled the legislature again. This time, they pushed through a law creating $10,000 for grants for kids in Utah to plant trees. When children match the grant money (state and national) with money they collect and contribute, they will plant over $27,000 worth of trees.

Another 10-year-old got an even heavier idea. "Why don't we find some money and make grants for kids across the nation to plant trees?" Audrey suggested, twirling a curl around her finger.

The children worked with their Senator, Orrin Hatch, to create a national fund for trees. Audrey attended the United Nations Youth Environment Forum in New York City and passed a petition asking the federal government to make a special fund for kids to plant trees. She collected over 1,500 signatures from kids around the nation. Then she flew to Washington, D.C., to deliver her petition and to lobby senators in person.

When Audrey returned to Salt Lake City, she and her Jackson friends wrote letters to every senator in Congress, asking for their support. Although Congress did not write a special bill for them, they did attach the idea to make money available for kids to the "America the Beautiful Act of 1990" (technically called The Food, Agriculture, Conservation and Trade Act of 1990—S2830).

Thanks to the Jackson kids, the bill now states that "youth groups" may apply for matching grants to plant trees. There will be federal money available for *you* to plant trees in *your* state.

Now, you're probably saying something like, "Yeah, but those Jackson kids are famous. I'm just a regular kid. I can't do all that." If you're a disbeliever, let me assure you. I'm their teacher, and I'll tattle on them. They sometimes forget assignments. They lose papers. Their bedrooms aren't always clean (not even Heather's). They're kids just like you, kids with dreams, kids who care. They're not rich or unusually clever. In fact, their school has the lowest income per capita (per person) in the Salt Lake School District.

But one thing they do have is courage. They don't give up easily. They believe that the future depends on them. They're not afraid to attack things that other people say can't be done.

As Heather says, "Big things can happen in small steps." ◉

Ten Tips for Taking Social Action

> ❝ **Basic research is what I'm doing when I don't know what I'm doing.** ❞
>
> *Werner von Braun*

You've read about the Jackson kids. Anything they can do, you can do, too. Here are ten steps that will lead you to your goal.

1. CHOOSE A PROBLEM. Look around your neighborhood. Are there any areas which look neglected or need improvements? Are there places that make you feel unsafe? Places that smell awful? Any problems with drugs, crumbling buildings, homeless people, hungry children, dangerous street crossings, grungy landscapes?

This is one good way to begin. You could also find a problem by thinking about a subject you have studied at school or in a scout troop. For example, if you have just finished a unit on mammals, you might ask yourself, "What kinds of problems do animals have or cause in real life?" If you can't think of anything, you might call your local humane society, animal shelter, or research clinic.

The hard part won't be finding a problem. The hard part will be choosing only *one* problem at a time.

2. DO YOUR RESEARCH. If you should find a problem from something you have studied at school, you already have valuable information to use. But try some new ways of researching, too.

Survey your school or neighborhood to find out how other people feel about the problem you selected. Telephone officials for information, then interview them over the phone or in person. Write letters. Read magazines and newspapers. If you happen to be a veteran couch potato, flip the TV to a news channel.

In Part Two: Power Skills, you'll learn more ways to do research.

3. BRAINSTORM POSSIBLE SOLUTIONS AND CHOOSE ONE. Think of what you might do to solve your problem. Brainstorm everything you can think of. Sometimes the zaniest ideas turn out to be the best.

You might try several solutions, or you might select only one. Choose solutions which seem the most possible and which will make the most difference.

4. BUILD COALITIONS OF SUPPORT. A *coalition* is a group of people working together for the same goal. Find all the people you can who agree with your solutions. Survey your neighborhood; ask teachers, city officials, newspapers, legislators, other students. Call state agencies that deal with your problem.

This is *very* important to do. Organize all these people. The more people you have on your team, the more power you will have to make a difference.

5. IDENTIFY YOUR OPPOSITION. In other words, find out who the "bad guys" are, or which people are against your solution. Only they might not really be "bad guys"—just people with different opinions.

Try to flush them out by asking teachers where your opposition might be, or questioning any other expert you can think of. Meet with your opponents to try to win them over to your ideas. Or you might compromise and work together. Always be polite and appreciate other opinions.

6. ADVERTISE. Here's good news: Television, radio, and newspaper reporters love stories of kid action. TV and radio stations usually offer free air time for worthy projects.

Call and ask to speak to a reporter who covers educational issues. Or you might write a letter. Be sure to include a phone number (yours?) the reporter can call for more information. Or send out a news release.

Don't forget small community newspapers, even church bulletins. They can help you advertise, too.

If you let people know what problem you're trying to solve, and what solution you propose, you'll suddenly find all sorts of people who want to climb aboard.

7. RAISE MONEY. After letting people know about your project, you might try to raise funds to support it. This isn't essential, and many wonderful projects can be tackled without this step. But sometimes you have more power if you put money where your mouth is.

8. CARRY OUT YOUR SOLUTION. You have your lineup of team players, and you've advertised to let people know the problem you plan to solve. Now DO IT!

Make a list of all the steps you need to take. Give speeches, write letters and proclamations, pass petitions, improve your neighborhood, campaign for world peace (or you might just try to spiff up your own backyard).

9. EVALUATE. Is your plan working? Are you congratulating yourself on your coolness, or do you feel more like you have a migraine headache? It's time to evaluate your project and its progress.

Have you tried everything? Should you change your solution? Do you need to talk with more people? It's up to you. You're in charge.

10. DON'T GIVE UP. Don't pay too much attention to folks who tell you all the reasons why your solution won't work. If you think your cause is really important, keep picking away at it.

Problem solving means weeding out all the things that don't work until you find something that does. Remember, a mountain looks tallest from the bottom. Don't give up. Climb!

> **❝ Luck is a matter of preparation meeting opportunity. ❞**
>
> *Oprah Winfrey*

WHAT'S YOUR PROBLEM?

Maybe you already know a problem you want to solve. Or maybe you're truly stuck on finding an issue to pursue.

On page 16, you'll find a list of areas from which you might brainstorm a problem. But first, let's review the Four Rules of Brainstorming:

1. Do it with a friend, your family, a group, or a class. The more brains you have to storm with, the more ideas you'll have. But you can also brainstorm alone.

2. Everybody tries to come up with as many ideas as possible—from silly to serious, and everything in between.

3. All ideas are acceptable during brainstorming. Make your choices later.

4. Nobody criticizes anybody else's ideas. Period. No exceptions!

You can brainstorm on blank paper, a chalkboard, or anything you choose. On this page and the next, you'll find examples of two filled-in brainstorming forms. The first is for writing down ideas. The second is for choosing an idea to work with, then making a plan of action.

If you like these forms, you'll find blank ones on pages 153 and 154 that you can copy and use.

BRAINSTORMING I: COME UP WITH IDEAS

idea-ideas

pollution — air, water, land, garbage

That makes me think of:
→ FACTORY STACKS / CAR EXHAUST
→ DRINKING WATER / HAZARDOUS WASTE
→ LANDFILLS

more wild & crazy ideas – KEEP GOING
- dioxin gas masks
- solar powered cars
- scrubbers on stacks
- lead in water pipes
- midnight dumping
- bacteria, germs
- fertilizer

idea-ideas

broken up sidewalk

→ SIDEWALKS MISSING - 8TH WEST
→ LACK OF CITY MONEY
→ NEIGHBORS DON'T CARE

- walk in streets
- elderly trip and get hurt
- people move away too fast

idea-ideas

grafitti, abandoned buildings, drugs, vandalism

→ GANGS / THE OLD PAINT FACTORY
→ THE CORNER AT 6TH WEST / NIGHT TIME
→ NEIGHBORS DON'T WATCH

- railroad station hides it
- dropouts
- lights broken or missing
- don't know each other

14

BRAINSTORMING II: CHOOSE YOUR MAIN IDEA

At this point, you have many ideas, some of them crazy. Now you should choose an idea to work on.

A. Ask yourself questions like: (1) Which idea might benefit the most people? (2) Which idea might have the best chance to succeed? (3) Which idea might cost the least to do? (4) Which idea might make the biggest difference? (5) Which idea do I like the best?

Think of questions which will help you make a good choice.

QUESTIONS

1. _Which idea might be the most possible to do?_
2. _Which idea do I like the best?_
3. _Which idea might help the most people?_
4. _Which idea might cost the least for us?_
5. _Which idea might help us learn the most?_

B. Choose one basic idea to work with:

We will encourage the repair of sidewalks in the Euclid area

C. Now list the steps to carry out your Plan of Action. Examples: Give speeches at the Community Council; write letters to the mayor; write a news release for TV and radio.

Then write down who will be responsible for each step, and when.

PLAN OF ACTION

ACTIVITY	WHO DOES IT?	WHEN?
Photo-survey of sidewalks	All of us	March 10
Call City Council	Gwen	March 7-11
Write speeches	Gwen, Sara, Donny, Dung, Errin	March 12-13
Speak to Mayor and City Council	" "	March 18
Call engineers	Sara	March 19
Write news releases	Donny, Errin	March 19
Meeting with engineers	All of us	March 30

What's the Problem?

Ask yourself that question for each of these topics. Decide which ones you might want to work with, or brainstorm topics of your own.

COMMUNITY CONCERNS

School
City growth and development; land use
Vacant lots, use of buildings
Beautification projects
Animals and wildlife
Garbage

SOCIAL CONCERNS

Family
Friends and social relationships
Human development
Population
Ethnic groups
Clothing
Shelter, abandoned houses
The homeless
Employment, unemployment
Public health, nutrition, hunger, mental health
Substance abuse (alcohol and other drugs, smoking)
Volunteerism
Support systems for children, the elderly, etc.

GOVERNING AGENCIES

Transportation
Law enforcement and justice
Education
Business and labor
Lawmaking agencies and governments
Social agencies

THE ENVIRONMENT

Energy production, energy use
Natural resources
Pollution (air, water, land)
Weather
Garbage

TECHNOLOGY AND SPACE

Communication
Information (microchips, etc.)
Satellites and space probes
Medicine, medical research
Industrial advances
Other inventions and projects
The future of technology and space

VALUE SYSTEMS

Money
Economic growth
Human rights
Ethics (morals and beliefs)
Religion
Censorship
Trade
Value systems throughout history

PUBLIC SAFETY

Peace
Weapons and gun control
Safety and accidents (including industrial)
Terrorism
Disasters (earthquakes, floods, fires, storms, etc.)
Disease

LEISURE TIME

Sports
Games
Recreation
Vacations
Hobbies
Styles and trends

❝ Activism pays the rent on being alive and being here on the planet...If I weren't active politically, I would feel as if I were sitting back eating at the banquet without washing the dishes or preparing the food. It wouldn't feel right. ❞

Alice Walker

Around the World

You can start taking social action in your own backyard or neighborhood. But you don't have to stop there. Many kids are literally changing the world.

In Sweden, a group of school children began an international effort to save the Costa Rican rain forest.

Scout groups everywhere have been busy tackling community problems. In Fiji, scouts turned a piece of neglected coastal land into a beautiful green space for local people and tourists to enjoy. Others in Indonesia re-greened an area serving over 25,000 villagers after it was devastated by a fire. In Central Java, scouts constructed a pipeline to bring fresh water for drinking and for watering rice fields to more than 11,000 people in four different villages. And in the Netherlands, scouts and local politicians joined to organize 25,000 scouts for a tree-planting project in 500 European cities.

Scout troops aren't the only young people who are making a difference worldwide. A youth leader in Kenya, Africa, operates out of a bus to organize and take volunteers into the field. She has involved over 500 students and local people in conservation and other worthwhile projects. Not too far away, in Zambia, one young volunteer organized a barefoot troupe of actors in performing anti-poaching plays to different villages. He wanted to discourage the wasteful killing of animals for their skins and for fun.

In Scotland, young volunteers ages 12 and up go off on one- to two-week conservation camps to improve the outdoors. A hop across the continent will take you to Germany, where 5,000 students wrote essays on environmental topics, then became involved in many local volunteer improvement projects.

Around the globe in Bangkok, Thailand, 74 young people from 28 youth organizations met on World Environmental Day to make plans for informative workshops.

The Soviets and Americans have joined forces in youth movements. U.S./U.S.S.R. Youth Environment Camps have met at Lake Tahoe in California and Lake Baikal in South Central Siberia. Kids from all over the world are invited to join in these annual programs.

Students at Sunnyside Elementary in Marysville, Washington, have adopted a stream, helped save salmon, and formed a partnership with a sister school, ligura Elementary, in Tokyo, Japan.

Does it make you tired just reading about the things these kids are doing? Or does it light a fire under you? If you're one of the fireballs, you can contact some of these international groups through the United Nations Environment Program (UNEP). You'll find their address and phone number on page 140. ◉

❝ It's a small world, but I wouldn't want to paint it. ❞

Stephen Wright

POWER SKILLS

POWER TELEPHONING

For many kids, the telephone is essential to a well-rounded social life. But did you know you can also use it to organize and collect information, interview people, take surveys, or even to lobby someone? You can save a lot of time if you let your fingers do the walking.

The telephone is the most basic communication tool we have, yet telephones in schools are practically kept under police protection. To use them sometimes requires a letter of permission from your parents (or an act of Congress). However, if you're working on a problem at school with other classmates, your teacher can usually get permission for you to use the guarded phones.

If you're a not a phone-call veteran, copy and fill out the phone form on page 155 before making your call. This will put many needed facts in front of your nose, like the name of your contact (the person you're calling) and your name. (That's right, *your* name, just in case your brain closes up shop when you get an important official on the phone.)

You'll also have your return address and phone number. Most people (not all) know their home address, but if you're calling from your school or club, you may not have that address memorized. If your contact wants to mail information to you, he or she might be too busy to wait while you hunt around for an address.

Finally, you'll have written down what you plan to say or ask. And you'll have a place to write down what your contact tells you.

Most Telephone Directories Have Three Sections

☞ The *blue* pages list government agencies or departments

☞ The *yellow* pages list businesses, associations, clubs, groups, etc.

☞ The *white* pages list people, plus many things also found in the yellow pages.

HOWEVER...

☞ In bigger cities, the white and blue pages may be published together in one directory, the yellow pages in another.

☞ The color codes might change from city to city. Watch for this if you need to use many different directories to track down your contacts.

Telephoning Tips

1. Get permission to use phones at your home, school, group, or club. It might sound routine, but it's important.

2. Copy and fill out the phone form on page 155, unless you're a seasoned phone buff.

3. When someone answers your call, state your name, grade, and school or organization. Even if you're doing a project on your own, you'll probably get better service if you mention your school name.

4. If you don't know the name of a contact, ask for someone in public relations or public information. This will usually land you in the right department.

5. If your contact isn't there, ask when he will be there. Write down the time. Call back at that time. Or leave your name, grade, school or organization, a phone number, a time when he can reach you, and a brief message about why you're calling. Most officials will return calls.

6. What if your contact doesn't call you back? Bug him! Call again and again. Persist until you get the information you need, but always be polite. Never

IMPORTANT
●●●●●●●●●
Never leave your home phone number or address without permission from your parents.

speak rudely. It will only hurt your cause. Remember, it's not your problem if someone else is rude. But don't worry. Most officials will think you're terrific.

7. When your contact does answer the phone, tell him your name, grade, and school or organization again. Then move on to the purpose of your call—what you want to say or ask.

8. Write down exactly what your contact tells you. You might have to ask him to repeat things. Most people talk faster than you can write.

Even though you may be able to instantly memorize stats on every player in the National Football League, you'll probably forget details of your phone conversation within five minutes of hanging up. So write it down!

9. While you have your contact on the phone, get his correct name, title, address, ZIP code, and phone extension. You may have talked to several people on

kids *in action*

Alison Stieglitz

Miami, Florida. Can one person make a difference? "You bet," says Alison Stieglitz. She began a project to feed the hungry on Thanksgiving Day, when she was only 13 years old.

"I wanted to help other people, and I felt that I could because of the money I got for my bat mitzvah," she explains. Taking the money given to her in honor of the religious ceremony, Alison assembled 15 baskets of food, including turkeys, which she passed out to elderly home-bound people for Thanksgiving dinner.

By the time she was 17, Alison had expanded her dream to include over 120 baskets. With each basket feeding four, that represents dinners for 480 people.

But she didn't stop at that. Throughout the past few years, she has made hundreds of phone calls and written "baskets" full of letters requesting funds from family members, friends, and community contacts. After incorporating the Thanksgiving Basket Fund into an official mini-business, she recruited many volunteers to help prepare and deliver the food baskets. She also serves as the only teenage member on the advisory board of the Family Counseling Center.

This all sounds pretty impressive. But if you talk to Alison, she sounds just like the girl next door. She worries about friends and what's going to be on the history test the next day. She downplays her volunteer work.

There's more to her story. Alison became one of the original organizers of the Hungry and Homeless committee in the Beth Am Temple. Since soup kitchens were closed on Sundays, she worked with two temples to establish a program to feed the homeless on that day. This organization now serves breakfast and bag lunches each Sunday to over 250 people.

your way to the right person. Maybe the first person put you on hold, then switched you to another person, who switched you to another person...You don't want to go through that all over again.

10. Leave your name, address, and phone number with your contact, so he can get in touch with you again.

11. When you have the information you need, thank your contact, then hang up.

12. File the phone form where you can find it again.

There's still more to Alison's story. This young woman has also adopted a shelter for abused and abandoned teenagers. Since she is editor of her high school newspaper, she writes a column encouraging other kids to go to the shelter to play games and make friends with the troubled teens.

Alison has received many awards of appreciation. She traveled to Washington to receive the Kleenex "Bless You Award," was given $2,000, and—you guessed it—donated it to the shelter.

Ask Alison if one person can make a difference, and she'll say, "Any small amount of effort or caring can make a large difference in people's lives." ◉

Alison Stieglitz prepares a Thanksgiving food basket.

Courtesy Sheila Stieglitz

POWER LETTER WRITING

> ## " The pen is mightier than the sword. "
>
> ### *Edward Bulwer-Lytton*

Have you ever really thought about what that saying means? When it comes to persuading people to action, good writing is better than using force. Good writing can change history.

You can have a great deal of power to make a difference in the world if you learn to write effective letters. And the best way to learn is to *do it*.

There are many different kinds of letters. Here are six:

1. INFORMATIONAL LETTERS gather information or give information to someone else.

2. SUPPORT LETTERS thank people or tell them that you agree with them.

3. PERSUASIVE LETTERS try to influence someone. For example, you might write to a legislator to ask her to support a bill.

4. OPPOSITION LETTERS tell people that you don't agree with them. For example, you might write to your governor to tell him you don't agree with the way the state is spending money.

5. PROBLEM/SOLUTION LETTERS identify a problem or propose a solution. For example, you might write to a newspaper editor stating the need for a larger zoo, a library, or an improved highway system.

6. REQUEST LETTERS ask for someone's help, encouragement, or support for a project you're involved in. You'll find an example on the next page.

Dear Sirs,

My name is Nikona Keller. I'm an E.L.P. student at Hawthorne Elementary School in the Salt Lake City School District. We have organized a group called KOPE (Kids Organized to Protect Environment). We have been meeting for five months. We first started with our own school grounds, planting gardens and trying to clean up the trash. Next we moved into the community and worked with Newspaper for Trees to recycle newspapers and cans. We worked all summer planning activities and helping in booths; we even made up one of our own called Tin-Toss. Other schools have asked us how to do this and so we would like to make newsletters and comic books to send to them to show them how to start it in their schools.

The money from our booths and other activities isn't going to last very long. We know that there are grants which teachers and other adults can apply for. Would you be interested in starting a grant program which school kids with good projects could apply for?

Thank you for listening.

Sincerely,

Nikona Keller

Nikona Keller

Hawthorne
School

How to Write a Letter to the Editor

Imagine how much fun it would be to see your writing in your neighborhood or city newspaper! You can do it. It isn't that hard. Your ideas could reach hundreds of thousands of people in a state-wide newspaper—many more in a national magazine. It's a great way to advertise and to make people aware of your problem.

Here are 12 tips for writing a letter to the editor that will enhance your chances of getting published. The two letter forms on pages 156 and 157 will help you to arrange the parts correctly. The form on page 156 shows you what to put where. The form on page 157 is blank so you can copy it and use it for your own letters.

1. Look for any rules printed in the magazine or newspaper you plan to write to. (Often these are found at the end of the Letters column.) Or call the newspaper on the phone to ask for special instructions.

2. For extra clout, write on school stationery.

3. If possible, type your letter or write it on a computer. But don't worry if you can't type or don't have access to a computer. You can hand write your letter, as long as it's neat and readable. Double-space your letter for easy reading, even if it's handwritten.

4. Include your return address and signature. Editors won't print your name if you ask them not to, but they probably won't print anonymous letters, either.

5. Start your letter like this:

To the Editor:

And end it like this:

Sincerely,

(Your Signature)
(Your Name Typed or Printed)
(Your Grade, School, or Organization)

Nothing fancy, nothing mushy, nothing too difficult.

6. Make sure that your letter is brief and clear. Don't repeat yourself. Editors aren't impressed with long-winded letters.

❝ I have made this letter longer than usual, because I lack the time to make it short. ❞

Blaise Pascal

7. Your subject matter should be something that's "in" or of current interest.

8. Never accuse anyone of anything without proof, or write anything libelous that could get you into trouble. (*Libel* makes someone look bad unfairly. People can get sued for libel.) Remember: you want to solve problems, not be a problem.

9. If you're writing because you think something should be done, give a few short reasons why.

10. Never send an "open letter," addressed to some public official, to a newspaper or magazine. It will probably end up in the editor's circular file (wastebasket).

11. Don't send the same letter to more than one newspaper. You probably wouldn't appreciate receiving a form letter from a friend. Newspapers like original work, too.

12. Proofread your letter for mistakes before sending it. But don't worry: your letter doesn't have to be perfect. The editor will make any needed corrections. The letter on this page shows some editor's corrections.

Also, you should know that letters are often shortened to fit the space available in the newspaper or magazine. Don't be surprised or upset if this happens to your letter.

January 5, 1989

Editor
Deseret News
Salt Lake City, Utah

~~Dear~~ **To the** Editor:

I like the comics section of the Deseret News very much, but lately I have become upset with the comic strip, "Boomers Song". The last few days "Boomers Song" has been making fun of homeless people.

I feel that the author, David Horsey, is very inconsiderate to ridicule these unfortunate people. I do not find it the least bit amusing or entertaining. The problem of the homeless is extremely serious and these people need to be helped, not mocked.

Stacey Miller
Stacey Miller
Age 14
Bountiful

How to Write a Letter to a Public Official

Should *you* write a letter to the mayor, the governor, a senator, even the President? Of course you should, if you have something to say. Follow the tips for writing a letter to the editor on pages 27–28, with these added hints. Copy and use the letter forms on pages 156 and 157 if you need help deciding what goes where.

1. The best time to write to a legislator is a month or so before the legislative session begins. She has more time to read your letter then. A week or so after you send your letter, call the legislator on the phone to jar her memory.

2. Make sure that your letter includes your return address, so your legislator can write back to you.

3. State your purpose in the first sentence. If you're writing to support or oppose a bill, identify it by number and name at the beginning.

4. Stick with one issue per letter. Don't try to wipe out air pollution, improve the budget, start a light-rail transit system, and save the whales all at once.

5. You probably hate writing school assignments that require a certain number of words (you spend more time counting than writing). You'll be glad to know that letters to officials should be as short as possible—only a few paragraphs, at the most—while still getting your point across.

6. It's okay to disagree with a public official, but do it politely. Never write a rude letter, and never threaten.

7. If possible, be complimentary. It never hurts to include a comment about something good the official has done. She'll be more willing to listen to a complaint or suggestion if you start off on a positive note.

8. It's not necessary to apologize for taking the official's time. Listening to people—including you—is her job. She might be surprised to get a letter from a kid, but that could work in your favor.

9. If you write to a legislator other than the one who represents your area, send a copy of your letter to your own representative. That's good manners, and your representative may want to help you, too.

You'll find examples of a real letter and response on the next two pages.

Jackson Elementary
750 W. 200 N.
SLC Utah 84116

March 17, 1989
The Honorable Mayor Palmer De
Paulis
The office of the Mayor
324 South State
Salt Lake City, Utah 84111

Dear Mayor De paulis:

We would like to be involved
in repairing cracked and distorted
sidewalks in the Euclid area.
I would like to see the sidewalks
repaired because of how bad it
makes the Euclid area look, I, Myself
have seen the sidewalks, and they aren't
a very nice sight. My friend and I
were walking down to a park in
the Euclid area And my friend
tripped on some rocks and scraped
her leg up So I would really
appreciate it if the sidewalks
were repaired
Sincerely,
Krista Crawford Fifth grade Ely

SALT LAKE CITY CORPORATION

DEPARTMENT OF PUBLIC WORKS
City Engineering Division
444 SOUTH STATE STREET
SALT LAKE CITY, UTAH 84111
535-7871

PALMER DePAULIS
MAYOR

MAX G. PETERSON, P.E.
CITY ENGINEER

April 17, 1989

Barbara Lewis and Students
E.L.P. Program
Jackson Elementary
750 West 200 South
Salt Lake City, Utah 84116

Dear Ms. Lewis and Students:

After receiving your letters regarding sidewalk conditions in the
Euclid area, I asked the City Engineering Division to conduct an
investigation. They have informed me of the meeting held with
all of you at Jackson Elementary on April 12, 1989. Your
sincerity and interest in civic affairs was very impressive to
our Engineering representatives.

We do appreciate your concerns and every effort will be made to
alleviate sidewalk problems in the Euclid area through future
Capital Improvement Program projects.

Sincerely,

Palmer De Paulis

Palmer Depaulis
Mayor of Salt Lake City

PD:LJ:kg

cc: Joseph R. Anderson
      Lynn Jarman
      Vault File 1-Z

31

Power Addresses

Here are some official addresses, plus examples of how you should start and end your letters. If you don't know the names and addresses of your own senators, representatives, governor, and mayor, ask your teacher or call your public library.

PRESIDENT OF THE U.S.

The President
The White House
Washington, D.C. 20500

    Dear Mr. President:
    Very respectfully yours,

VICE PRESIDENT

The Vice President
The White House
Washington, D.C. 20500

    Dear Mr. Vice President:
    Very respectfully yours,

MEMBER OF THE PRESIDENT'S CABINET

The Honorable Caspar W. Weinberger
The Secretary of Defense
Washington, D.C. 20301

    Dear Mr. Secretary:
    (If a woman, Dear Madam Secretary:)
    Sincerely yours,

U.S. SENATOR

The Honorable Barbara Covey
United States Senate
Washington, D.C. 20510

    Dear Senator Covey:
    Sincerely yours,

U.S. REPRESENTATIVE

The Honorable Timothy J. Penny
House of Representatives
Washington, D.C. 20515

    Dear Mr. Penny:
    Sincerely yours,

GOVERNOR

The Honorable Michael O. Leavitt
Governor of Utah
State Capitol, Room 210
Salt Lake City, Utah 84114

    Dear Governor Leavitt:
    Sincerely yours,

MAYOR

The Honorable Mayor Palmer DePaulis
The Office of the Mayor
450 South State Street
Salt Lake City, Utah 84111

    Dear Mayor DePaulis:
    Sincerely yours,

(Use this form for letters to your commissioner, too.)

WORLD LEADER

(Name of World Leader)
(Country) Embassy
United Nations
United Nations Plaza
New York, New York 10017

Carl Sandburg Junior High

Levittown, Pennsylvania. This story about eight ninth graders at Carl Sandburg Junior High is especially nice because it didn't cost anything and still made a difference.

The students told their story in their entry to the Future Problem Solving Contest. Here is part of what they wrote:

> *The kids in our class...were very upset about the...millions of acres [that] were burning In Yellowstone National Park in Wyoming [Fall, 1988]. From the reports in newspapers and on television, the people...thought Yellowstone was burning to the ground. We thought most of the animals were dead...We couldn't figure out why the Park Service wouldn't fight the fires until after they had already burned for weeks.*

Dubbing themselves "The Forest Healers," these eight kids wrote to their representatives in Congress and corresponded with the Department of the Interior. They were totally surprised with the answers they received. Among many other valuable facts, they learned that allowing forests to burn is a natural healing process which releases nutrients into the soil and helps certain seeds to sprout. This process repeats itself every two or three centuries.

The Forest Healers began an information campaign to teach elementary school children about the importance of this type of forest fire. They created a poster contest for younger children and wrote to the administration at Yellowstone, asking for their cooperation with the contest.

Next, these student organizers wrote a play. Dressed in homemade costumes—cardboard flower petals, floppy rabbit ears, and a crinkly red cape for the fire—they performed the play at three schools. They told the children about their contest. Everyone who entered received a special Poster Recognition Award with "Poppy, the Pinecone" smiling from the center. The winning posters were mailed to Yellowstone for display in the park.

You'll find the students' letter to Yellowstone and an example of the Poster Recognition Award on the next two pages. ◉

The Forest Healers perform their play about forest fires.

Courtesy John Rock

FOREST HEALERS
c/o John Rock
Carl Sandburg Junior High School
Harmony Road
Levittown, PA 19056

Superintendent,
P.O. Box 168
Yellowstone National Park, WY 82190
Re. Park Rehabilitation and Recovery Program

Dear Sir or Madam:

We are a group of ninth grade students who were so alarmed by the reports of the fires last summer and fall that we sent a letter to our congressman urging him to do something to allow us to help Yellowstone recover. Our congressman sent our letter to the Department of the Interior.

The information we received from the National Park Service over the past few months made us understand that the fires were in some ways beneficial to the environment of the park, and that fires are a part of the natural process.

We have decided to organize a project that will help other students understand how forest fires act as a part of the natural process. Our project involves performing a skit for elementary school students, and then running a poster contest in these elementary schools, in which the students will illustrate the beneficial effects of forest fires.

The purpose of our skit is to educate the elementary students and to arouse interest in the poster contest. We have already begun to work on ideas and characters for the skit. We have designed a main character that is a pine cone. We have not yet decided on a name for him or her, but we have enclosed a picture of the character. The pine cone character will be the symbol we will use on the certificates we will award to the students who enter the contest.

We would like to tell the students that the winning posters will be sent to Yellowstone Park to be displayed there. Would you be willing to do this? Also, would you be willing to return the posters if we paid for the return postage?

One of the reasons we thought about the display idea is that visitors to the park might be motivated to make posters of their own on the same theme, or even to organize poster contests in their own schools or churches or scout organizations. In this way, many others might be educated. Would you be willing to encourage such an activity?

Sincerely,

Melissa Mather, Donna Winter,
Heather Smith, Michael Barsky,
Wendell Buck, Keith Bogart,
Gordon Foster, Brian Sullivan

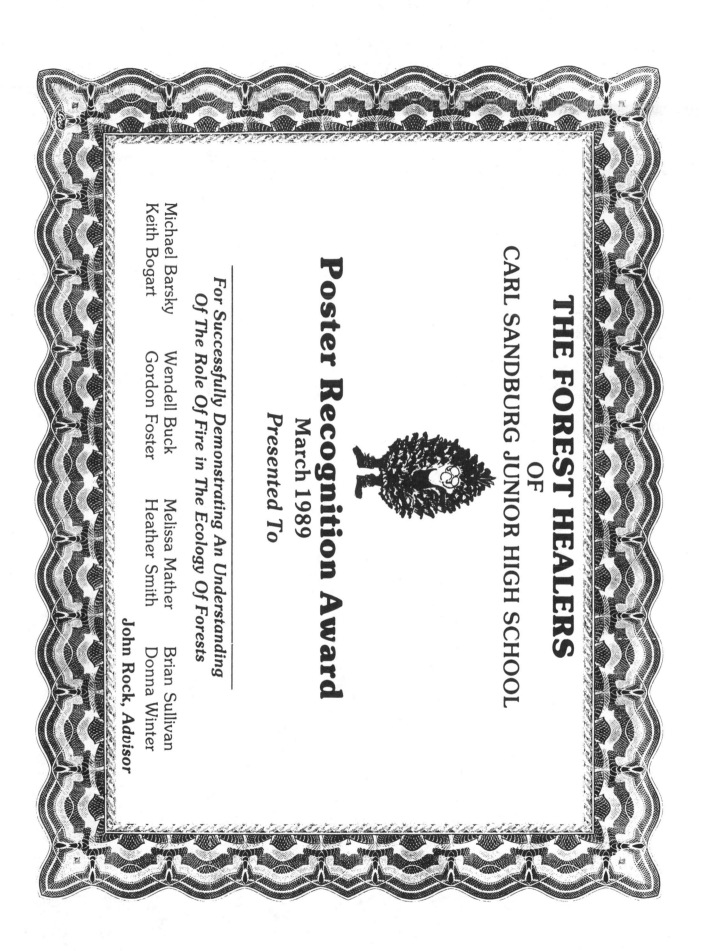

THE FOREST HEALERS

OF

CARL SANDBURG JUNIOR HIGH SCHOOL

Poster Recognition Award

March 1989

Presented To

For Successfully Demonstrating An Understanding
Of The Role Of Fire in The Ecology Of Forests

Michael Barsky	Wendell Buck	Melissa Mather	Brian Sullivan
Keith Bogart	Gordon Foster	Heather Smith	Donna Winter

John Rock, *Advisor*

Bellamy Middle School

Chicopee, Massachusetts. Chicopee had a sludge problem. What's sludge? The liquid wastes collected from factories and public buildings, plus sewage from homes. Chicopee's problem happened when the state of Massachusetts ordered a halt on burning the sludge because it violated air quality regulations. Winter came, and the sludge froze before it could be hauled to landfills. Officials suggested building a brick building around the sludge to keep it warm. The cost? About $120,000, which the city didn't have.

Kids to the rescue! Those in the Reach program at Bellamy Middle School read about the problem in the newspaper. They visited the sludge plant to get a close-up view (not to mention a close-up smell).

Pulling her jacket tightly to keep the falling snow off her shoulders, eighth grader Renee Cusson asked the guide, "What do you do with all this garbage in a rainstorm?"

"It gets pretty messy," the engineer admitted.

Back at Bellamy, the kids researched and brainstormed possible solutions. Then they reached out to the community with a proposal for a better solution. They mailed a letter to the chief operator of the plant with their suggestions, which included building a 20-foot by 12-foot makeshift solar greenhouse to keep the sludge warm in the winter. The cost? Only $5,000—a savings to the city of $119,500.

"I just thought that they had to raise the temperature to keep the sludge from freezing," seventh grader Matthew Goff explains. "The most efficient way was to use the natural energy of the sun."

Their idea worked so well that city officials scrapped the idea for a brick building. The solar room will remain a permanent "temporary" solution.

As eighth grader David P. Blood says, "It made me feel really good to know that we had an effect." ◉

Bellamy Middle School students David Blood, Eric Boudreau, Matthew Goff, Heather Simonich, and Melissa Goodenough

POWER INTERVIEWING

> ## **"Opinion...is but knowledge in the making. "**
>
> *John Milton*

Where do you usually go when you need information? Books? Magazines? Newspapers? Your library? Those are all good sources, but reading is just one way of gathering information. You can learn a great deal from talking with an expert.

And if you need really current information, an interview is better than a book. Books sometimes take a year or more to produce, but an interview is *now*. Besides, interviewing someone can be fun. It's exciting to chat with a person face-to-face.

There are many different types of interviews. Here are four you can try.

1. INFORMATION GATHERING INTERVIEWS are fact-finding missions to learn more about your problem.

2. PERSONALITY PORTRAITS help you paint "word pictures" about famous people or experts. What makes them tick? Find out.

3. OPINION GATHERING INTERVIEWS are like surveys, but you can find out much more information, and you get to know the person besides.

4. PERSUASIVE INTERVIEWS help you build coalitions of support. Talk about the problem you're tackling. Try to convince the person to help you. You will have more power if you can convince some important people to join your team.

Interviewing Tips

1. Call or write to set up an appointment. (The phone is faster.)

2. Make a list ahead of time of four or five questions to ask. Other friends or a teacher can help you think of some.

Don't take a whole suitcase of questions to ask. Leave some room in the interview for spontaneous questions and answers.

3. Copy and use the interview form on page 158. Record the name, title, phone number, and address of the person you will be interviewing.

Write your questions on the form, if you like, and number them. During the interview, use extra paper to write the answers. Don't try to write them under the questions. You won't know how much space you'll need. Instead, identify your answers with the same numbers you gave the questions.

After the interview, record the date and the starting and ending times.

4. Arrive at the interview on time.

5. If you have a tape recorder, you could take it along to record the interview. But you must get permission from the person you're interviewing. And it's still a good idea to take notes, writing down the most important ideas. If your notes are hard to decipher later, you can check the recorder for accuracy. (And if your recorder doesn't work for some reason, you'll have your notes.)

A tape recorder isn't essential. Some people prefer only notes.

6. If you have a camera, you could bring it and snap pictures. Again, you must get permission from the person you're interviewing. If there are products to photograph, this is especially enjoyable.

7. If you're a furious note-taker, don't forget additional paper. And plenty of extra, pre-sharpened pencils. (Get the point?)

8. If the person you're interviewing wants to go off on a tangent (in other words, wants to talk about something else besides the answers to your questions), let him. You might get some of your best information that way. Then return to your questions.

9. Remember that you're there to learn, not to impress the other person with how much you know. Good interviewers are good listeners, too.

10. Ask the person where he learned his information. That's a good way to check on the accuracy of what he's saying. And, of course, ask him where you can go to learn more.

11. If the person speaks too quickly for you to write his answers, politely ask him to repeat what he said.

12. You might want to invite the person to be a guest speaker in your class. Take a calendar along just in case.

13. Before you leave, thank the person for his time. And when you return home or to school, write a thank-you note and mail it right away. Not only is this polite, it also makes the person more anxious to help you again.

14. Organize your interview information in some way and present it to your class, a community council, or some other group whose members might be interested. *Share what you have learned.* This is the step where you can really make a difference.

IMPORTANT
• • • • • • • • •

Never go alone to an interview.

Always get a parent, teacher, or other adult to go with you.

Millsap Elementary

Cyprus, Texas. "Give two bits for the *Texas*," wrote the children from Millsap Elementary to every school in their state. The reason? The *Texas*, an old battleship which had served in two World Wars, was about to collapse. It had peeling paint and rusted-out holes big enough to thrust your fist through.

Other Texas children had rallied around the ship once before, back in 1948. Thinking she had served well and deserved a peaceful retirement, the kids saved the ship from becoming a target for bomb practice at the end of World War II. To bring the *Texas* home to Texas, they collected $12,000 in nickels.

The Millsap students decided that kids should save the beautiful old ship again. They blitzed across the community, interviewing everyone from the Texas Parks and Wildlife authorities to their own grandparents, collecting information and stories in their statewide children's campaign.

It was hard work, but their advisor, Cassie Johnson, told them to have confidence in themselves. Are you ready for the result? The project begun by the Millsap kids spread to private schools and colleges across the state. Together, the students raised over $100,000—enough to completely repaint the *Texas* inside and out. Not a bad retirement for their old salty friend. ◉

Millsap kids, on board the Texas, receive the Caspar Knight Award from the Association of Historic Naval Ships of North America.

Courtesy Cassie Johnson

POWER SPEECHES

Does your face have an acne attack at the mere thought of giving a speech? Or are you one of those kids who automatically migrates to the microphone to monopolize it? Either way, you can learn to give great speeches. You might be surprised at the attention officials will give to your ideas.

Tips for Successful Speeches

1. Choose the right audience to hear your speech. These should be people who would naturally be associated with or interested in the problem you're tackling—and people who have power to act on your ideas.

2. Remember "K-I-S-S," for "Keep It Short and Simple"? It works for letters, and it works for speeches, too. Short speeches are usually more powerful and memorable than long ones. One to five minutes is plenty.

3. Keep your speech from sounding "canned." After you finish writing it, jot down one or two words to remind you of each sentence or paragraph. Make a list of these words to take with you. (You can sneak a peek at these if you get a brain cramp when you're giving your speech.) Memorize ideas, not whole sentences.

Here's an example:

If your written speech says this:	write down and remember this:
"With all the air pollution we have in our city, trees can be a big help. One tree, in its average 50-year life, will clean up $62,000 worth of air pollution."	air pollution 1 tree = $62,000
"Cars contribute to air pollution with exhaust. Sometimes it seems like there are more cars on the road than there are people. Industrial stacks can pollute the air, too."	exhaust industrial stacks

4. Practice delivering your speech by yourself at first, until you feel comfortable. Deliver it to a wall. (Walls make very quiet audiences and hardly ever talk back or criticize.) When you feel more secure, practice with a friend or family member.

5. Will you be nervous before giving your speech? Probably. Most people chew their nails down before getting in front of an audience. Since you're a kid, however, no one will expect your speech to be perfect. And when you deliver it, just imagine that you're talking to your family and friends. It will help you to speak in a more natural way.

> **Try hard for a good opener and closer. Then make sure they're close together.**
>
> *M. Dale Baugham*

6. Look at your audience when you speak. Keep your chin up and smile. The most important thing you have to sell is yourself.

7. If you're interrupted by noise, wait until it's quiet before starting to speak again.

8. It may seem to you as if you're shouting into a megaphone, but speak loudly and slowly. If you speak into a microphone, hit it dead center with your voice.

9. Make your speech interesting. Tell a story, describe an experience, quote an expert, shock your audience with a statistic. You may want to show slides, a video, a chart, or a graph. If you use any of these things, make sure they're big enough for the whole audience to see.

10. Leave time for questions and answers at the end. Ten minutes or so should be enough.

11. If you really want to impress your audience, leave a one-page flyer listing the major points of your speech. And you may want to leave a phone number where you can be reached for more details.

You'll find examples of student speeches on the next page.

Jackson kids speak before the Salt Lake City Council to encourage sidewalk repair.

Barbara Lewis

SPEECHES DELIVERED TO CITY COUNCIL AND
MAYOR PALMER DE PAULIS
(To Solicit Sidewalk Repairs in the Euclid Area)

Jackson Elementary
Salt Lake City, Utah
March, 1989

SARA: My name is Sara Aguila. We are from Jackson Elementary fifth grade Extended Learning Program. We went on two surveys in the Euclid area to look at the sidewalks, and we found that:

1. Elderlies might fall or someone else.
2. People think the sidewalks are SO BAD they would rather walk on the street.
3. Some people don't know where the sidewalk is, or there isn't one there.
4. There are pebbles and rocks loose.

Will you please help us?

GWEN: My name is Gwen Warner. I used to deliver the *Deseret News*. When my brother and I had to walk the route, we had to walk in the streets, because it was safer and easier than the sidewalks! Even when I walked on the sidewalks, I tripped a lot because of the way the sidewalks were!

We would really like to see the Euclid area improved, because children could fall and hurt themselves while playing around there.

Please help and improve the Euclid area.

DUNG: My name is Dung. I went on a sidewalk survey, too. I'd like to say something. The old people can't even walk on the sidewalk. There's a lot of business traffic, and if old people can't walk on the sidewalk, they might get hit. They have to walk on the street, and cars don't see them, because old people are short!

DONNY: Ladies and gentlemen, my name is Donald Seher, and I have something to say, also. And I must say that Big Foot and the Abominable Snowman couldn't go over the sidewalks. That area must have been a testing range for the Air Force.

Thank You For Your Time. Good-bye.

ERINN: Here are some pictures we took of the sidewalks. (He hands them to mayor.)

ALL: Thank you very much.

John Clark Hill

Homer, Georgia. When the doors to the new courthouse in Homer opened to the public, the historic Banks County Courthouse was scheduled for demolition. Sixteen-year-old John Clark Hill admired the beauty of the old building. He decided that was no way to treat a work of art, let alone a historic building which had been around so long it seemed like an old friend.

He took action to save it. He wrote editorials to local newspapers and gave speeches before the chamber of commerce, the historical society, and any other group which would listen, pleading for restoration.

When the Save the Courthouse committee was formed, Clark was chosen as chairman of the activities committee. He hit the public with bumper stickers, radio spots, and signs. The campaign worked. The old Courthouse was saved. When the renovations are finished, it will house art exhibits and a genealogy library, and serve as a civic center for plays and concerts. ◉

John Clark Hill in front of the courthouse he helped to save.

Courtesy John Clark Hill

Carla Derrick and Leslie Wilson

Chapin, South Carolina. It's hard to be a teenager. You worry whether you look good, whether other kids will like you, whether you will succeed in the future. But what if you had to cope with cancer, too?

Both Carla Derrick and Leslie Wilson were diagnosed with different types of cancer when they were only seven years old. Carla lost an eye to the disease; Leslie lost a lung and her left leg. Although death brushed their cheeks, they didn't give in.

"You come close to death, and you realize how much you have to live for," Leslie says. "You want to accomplish all you can in the time you have."

While she was in high school, Carla was chosen to attend the Governor's School for the Arts one summer. She was an active member of the student council, president of her theater club, and captain of her debate team. Leslie served as scorekeeper for the track team, as a student council member, and as student body vice president. Thanks to an artificial limb, she even dives, swims, and roller-skates.

But Carla and Leslie do more than that. They also give speeches and counsel other young people with cancer.

Today the cancer in both girls is in remission. And both are active members of a cancer support group called "Lasting Impressions," which is lobbying for legislation for insurance assistance for the terminally ill. Together they made a video titled "How to Cope," now being nationally distributed, which answers some of the questions newly-diagnosed teenagers with cancer often ask. Both girls helped to write, produce, and direct the video. They also appear in it as living proof that cancer can be fought and won.

"Cancer changed my life," Carla says. "I feel I'm a much better person because of it. I don't take life for granted. I try to see some good in everything, because there is good in everything...It was the hardest thing that I have ever had to go through, and I made it, and I'm not afraid of anything now."

To find out more about the "How to Cope" video, call (803) 434-3583. Leslie would especially like you to know that the Sabolich Prosthetics Research Center in Oklahoma City, Oklahoma, makes specially fitted, state-of-the-art artificial limbs which allow better mobility. For more information, call toll-free 1-800-522-4428, or write: Sabolich Prosthetics Research Center, P.O. Box 60509, Oklahoma City, OK 73146. ⊙

Carla Derrick (left) and Leslie Wilson (right).

Courtesy Pam Steude

44

POWER SURVEYS

When you collect opinions from people in a group or a neighborhood, you have a survey. What's the point? Because it's hard to say what's best for people without first finding out how *they* feel.

For example, maybe you think that all of the trees in your neighborhood should be painted blue. But when you survey your neighbors, they don't agree. You've learned that trying to go ahead with your project probably isn't a good idea.

Collecting people's opinions isn't the only way to conduct a survey. Some students at Jackson Elementary thought their neighborhood sidewalks should be repaired. They planned to ask the mayor of Salt Lake City for help. Since they didn't think the mayor would have time to come to see the sidewalks for himself, the students did a photographic survey. In other words, they took the sidewalks to the mayor! They showed the pictures to the mayor and his council. They gave short speeches. (You'll find their speeches on page 42.) Together, their speeches and pictures were very convincing. The result? The sidewalks were repaired.

Remember the Jackson kids who cleaned up the hazardous waste site? As part of their work on this problem, they surveyed their neighborhood, looking for wells. They thought they could ask health officials to take samples of the water from the wells to find out if it was contaminated.

What kinds of surveys could you conduct? Brainstorm ideas. For example: How do students at your school feel about the lunchroom, school rules, running for class offices? How do people in your neighborhood think garbage collection could be improved? How do they feel about recycling, beautification projects, and so on?

You'll learn that surveys do more than gather information. They help you build coalitions of support—people who agree with your ideas. They help you to identify your opposition—people who are against your ideas. What you learn from surveys might even change your opinions.

Professionals sometimes conduct surveys to try to find out how people will vote in an election. These are called *polls*. Have your parents ever participated in a poll?

Jackson kids conduct a sidewalk survey to encourage improvements near their neighborhood.

Barbara Lewis

45

❝ There are two sides to every question. 🗐

Protagoras

There are many different kinds of surveys. Here are three main types you could use. Which one you choose depends on what you're trying to do.

1. OPINION SURVEYS collect opinions of a group. Check out the example on this page.

2. INFORMATION SURVEYS collect information.

3. AWARENESS SURVEYS make people aware of a problem or situation. You can help shape people's opinions with awareness surveys.

❝ It's a very great thing to be able to think as you like. 🗐

Matthew Arnold

SAMPLE OPINION SURVEY
Animals in medical research

SA-strongly agree   A-agree   D-disagree   SD-strongly disagree

A 1. Animals should never be used in medical experimentation.
D 2. Pound seizure should be illegal.
A 3. The number of animals used in experimentation should be limited.
SA 4. Animals should only be used in medical research by state-approved research facilities.
SA 5. Research facilities must use anesthesia in all experiments with animals.

SAMPLE TABULATION OF RESULTS

	SA	A	D	SD	Undecided
1.	*15	14	17	14	10
2.	14	17	14	13	12
3.	16	14	12	14	14
4.	17	10	0	22	21
5.	20	39	11	0	0

* number of people who strongly agree with question #1.

Tips for Successful Surveys

Surveys can be done almost anywhere: in a school, a neighborhood, a scout troop, a shopping mall. For some places, you may need to get permission first.

Surveys can be done in almost any way: in person, by phone, or by mail. If you have access to a phone, this can really save time. The catch? Some people don't like to answer questions on the phone. Letters are great, but they take time to write, copy, and mail. And there's no guarantee that people will answer them. So if you really want to know what people think, get out and ask them.

1. If your survey will require you to travel away from home or school, get permission first. For surveys done on school time, or as part of a school project, you'll need to get permission slips signed by parents.

2. If you will be traveling in a school group, check to see if there are any district policies you have to follow.

3. You can travel by walking, by bus, or by car. If you travel by car, make sure that every adult driver has liability insurance and a seat belt for each kid.

4. You'll also need one or more adult supervisors or chaperons. Teachers, troop leaders, and parents are some possibilities.

IMPORTANT
• • • • • • • • •

Never do a neighborhood survey alone.

Always get a parent, teacher, or other adult to go with you.

---

5. If you think your survey might make a difference to your neighborhood or city, try getting some media coverage. TV and newspaper reporters might be interested in coming along when you conduct your survey. This is great, because media coverage can take your project to a much larger group of people than you could ever reach yourself. Find out more about media coverage on pages 66–77.

6. If you're normal kids who like to chat, your survey will probably take longer to conduct than you expect. So allow more time than you think you need.

7. If you're collecting information or opinions, be sure to organize your questions ahead of time. If possible, limit your questions to five or fewer.

Copy and use either of the survey forms on pages 159 and 160 to write your questions and record responses. The form on page 159 is for one person's responses to many questions. The form on page 160 can be used for many people's responses to fewer questions.

8. Some people you survey might challenge your questions and disagree with your solutions, if you share them. Keep calm and stay polite anyway. Never speak or act rudely.

9. Take plenty of paper (or survey forms) and extra pencils. In your enthusiasm, you're probably going to break a few leads. Who has time to run back to school or home to sharpen a pencil?

10. When you finish your survey, organize your findings in a chart, report, or visual. This is important. Otherwise, why did you do a survey?

You can copy and use the form on page 161 to tabulate your results and write comments about them. (What do you think they mean? Were you surprised by what you learned?)

11. Present your findings to one or more groups—other students, troops, your principal, clubs, community or parent groups. Present them to an agency connected with your problem. For example, when Jackson kids surveyed their school to find out which children had played on a hazardous waste site, they sent their results to the health department.

Don't skip this step. There's no point in doing a survey if you don't use the opinions and information you collect.

West Iredell High School

Statesville, North Carolina. How do friendly high school kids spend Friday night in a small town in the foothills of North Carolina? They climb into Chrysler convertibles with fur-lined seats, turn up their radios full blast, and cruise the local mall parking lot, looking for friends and cute guys or girls from one of the four area high schools.

Sound harmless? Not so, said local mall merchants, who shook their fists and complained at the 500 teens who cruised through their parking lot. The kids took up parking spaces and scared away shoppers, the merchants said. Police agreed. They placed extra officers on duty to patrol the cruisers and try to cut down on the fender benders. Local residents were miffed and stayed away, cutting down on mall business.

Enter the Community Problem Solving (CPS) team from West Iredell High School. With the encouragement of advisor, Karen Charles, these four kids—Lisa Dobson, Rikki Ashley, Rob Osborne, and Alex Wooten—brainstormed possible solutions to this heated town controversy. Rob and Alex circulated a survey among the juniors and seniors at the four high schools, asking if students would be willing to relocate their "cruisin'" to another area. (You can see their survey on the next page.) Eighty-seven percent responded with a resounding "yes."

This clever CPS team located an abandoned drive-in movie theater, whose owner agreed to allow the use of his hunk of concrete. High school kids also agreed to pay for admission.

The problem solvers met with local officials and merchants and presented their plan, which included forming a board of directors, making security arrangements, and organizing cleanup and maintenance teams. Then they wrote a letter to the editor of a local newspaper.

Unfortunately, the teens never got their slab of concrete. Their plan died, tangled up in bureaucratic red tape. Not everything you try works out the way you want it to.

Maybe the community didn't change too much, but the students did. And they never forgot the self-confidence they developed while working on their problem. For, you see, they're still cruisin'. When the end-of-the-year prom rolled around, these same kids collected $800.00 from classmates for a midnight "cruise" on Lake Norman on board the romantic ship, the *Catawba Queen*. They planned, organized, and advertised this special event.

"I never would have thought we could do this ourselves," said senior Rikki Ashley. But they did, and you can, too. ◉

Courtesy Karen Charles

John Daughtrey, Director, North Carolina/South Carolina Future Problem Solving; West Iredell Students Rob Osborne, Ryan Chappel, Rikki Ashley, and Lisa Dobson; Karen Charles, Advisor

Student Cruisin' Survey
(Circulated Through Four High Schools)

1. Do you cruise the mall?

Yes _____ No _____

2. Why do you cruise?

_____

_____

_____

_____

_____

3. If an area is made available, would you be willing to cruise somewhere else?

Yes _____ No _____

4. Would you be willing to pay an admission fee at a new site?

No _____ Yes _____; If "yes," which would you choose?

Per use fee _____ (like $1.00 per person).

Flat membership fee _____ (like $10.00 per season).

5. Would you like any of the following services at a new site?

Music _____ Arcade _____ Concessions _____

Other _____

_____

_____

_____

6. Would you object to security being provided at this site?

Yes _____ No _____

(Prepared by Rob Osborne, Alex Wooten, Lisa Dobson, Rikki Ashley, West Iredell High School, Statesville, North Carolina; advisor, Karen Charles.)

POWER PETITIONS

"No one listens to me!" How many times have you said that? It's a common complaint. But you can do something about it. You can collect other voices and create a louder noise—one that's harder for people to ignore.

A *petition* is a paper with signatures to prove that many people agree with your position. It's a demonstration of group strength. It can be a very powerful tool in gaining the attention you might need for your problem or project.

Jackson kids have written several petitions. They gathered signatures from residents around the barrel site asking for removal of the 50,000 barrels. They passed a petition, which they presented to the faculty, to gain permission to wear shorts in school during the last sweaty months before summer. (You can see this petition on the next page.) They passed around another petition asking for a sixth grade dance, and another to get permission to chew gum in school (this last one failed).

Jason Weaver, a seventh grade graduate from Jackson, passed a petition around his trailer court in an effort to get a caution light by his street. "You took your life in your hands every time you stuck your toe off the curb," he complained.

A group called Kids Against Pollution (KAP) in Closter, New Jersey, is circulating a national petition which advocates the adoption of state and national constitutional amendments to guarantee citizens' rights to clean water, air, and land.

There are many examples, and you can think of your own reasons for writing petitions. However, presenting your petition to the right group is just as important as collecting the signatures. You must ask yourself, "Which person or group would have the power to do something about my petition?"

Jackson kids petition to encourage cleanup of a hazardous waste site.

Courtesy Paul Barker, *Deseret News*

NOTE: The kind of petition described in this section is not the same as a *formal* petition to make a change in the government or to pass a law. A formal petition has certain requirements. You can read more about formal petitions on pages 99–101.

Petition

We the students of Jackson Elementary School would like to be able to wear shorts to school. The reasons for wearing shorts are:

It is very hot and some days gets to 90° (on an average 80°).

There is no air-conditioning.

It's very uncomfortable for the teachers and the students. We feel that we would be more comfortable if we didn't have to worry about how hot we are. We will be able to reason with you on some rules such as: not on crummy days or cold days, not wearing short shorts or tank tops or real short tops.

We think that if the students don't play and goof off with them, they can wear them, but if not that they won't be able to wear them for the next two weeks.

NAME	GRADE	ROOM
April Chacon	6th	23 Graves
Jamie Atwood	6th	23 Graves
hochann Juo	6th	23 graves
Josh Roy	6th	23 graves
Pete Borton	6th	27-Thompson
aaron Iversen	6th	23 Graves
Jason Weaver	6th	27 Thompson

Tips for Successful Petitions

Copy and use the petition form on page 162, or create a form of your own.

1. Most of the time, you'll want to use regular 8 1/2" x 11" paper to describe your problem and collect signatures. But this isn't essential. For example, if your problem is school restroom reform, you might make a stronger statement by collecting signatures on a roll of toilet paper.

2. Give your petition a title. (For example, "Petition for Traffic Safety.")

3. Identify your group.

4. Identify the official or agency who will receive your petition.

5. Write a statement describing the problem that's the reason for your petition, or the plan you're proposing. This should appear at the top of every petition page. (That's so people can't say they didn't understand what they were signing.)

6. Provide blank lines after your statement for people to write any or all of these:
   a. their signature
   b. their class, grade, or group
   c. their school or hometown
   d. their address and phone number

Some petitions might require addresses as proof that the signers are property owners in the area. Also, you might want to contact some of your signers again. Give people the choice of listing this information.

7. Number the signature lines for easy totaling.

IMPORTANT
●●●●●●●●●

If you plan to take your petition door-to-door, never go alone.

Always get a parent, teacher, or other adult to go with you.

---

8. Smile! The better you treat the people you meet, the more likely they'll sign your petition.

9. Some people you ask to sign your petition might disagree with you about your problem. Keep calm and stay polite anyway. Never speak or act rudely.

10. When you're through collecting signatures, photocopy all the pages of your petition. Keep the copy in a safe place. You may need proof of the signatures later, if your original petition is lost.

11. Present your petition to someone who has power to act on your ideas.

Rebecca Brown

Boyertown, Pennsylvania. Just about everyone has heard of Boyertown's winning American Legion baseball teams. The town has been wildly supportive and proud of their kids. But while Boyertown had great baseball, it didn't have a library.

High school student Rebecca Brown believed that books should be as important as baseball. She set about creating her own lineup of players until she had a team willing to fight for a town library. She made a hit speaking at civic groups, collected signatures on a petition, and brought the issue before the public by writing radio spots and newspaper articles. She and her Girl Scout troop applied for two grants, netting $850 for library books.

Their library, which began humbly with the troop running a Saturday morning children's story hour, grew as it gathered support from other groups. Finally, Rebecca's efforts resulted in a home run for books. The town purchased an old beauty salon and turned it into a real library. ◉

Rebecca Brown at the town library she helped to create.

Courtesy Ron Romanski, *Eagle/Times*

POWER PROPOSALS

Pretzels could be called "crackers without a plan." They double back, cross themselves out, and never arrive anywhere.

If you have a powerful idea, don't turn it into a pretzel. Get it out there, where other people can react to it and act on it. Make a plan. Write a proposal.

This is actually a lot simpler than it sounds. A proposal doesn't need signatures, like a petition. You can present it to any individual or group you want to influence. It gives your idea punch.

You might design proposals to start clubs, to change old school rules or add new ones, to set aside a special day to honor someone, to make an official aware of a problem, or anything else you choose. You'll find an example of a new club proposal on the next page.

Proposal Writing Tips

Copy and use the proposal form on page 163, or create a form of your own.

1. Give your proposal a title.

2. Name the audience you will present it to.

3. Identify your group.

4. Record the date.

5. Write a brief description.

6. Describe your plan of action, or how you will carry out your idea.

7. Write a needs statement which lists any equipment or services you will need.

8. Make a budget. This might include fundraising. (Learn about fundraising on pages 57–65.)

9. Include a time line of when your project will begin and how long it will continue.

10. If possible, present your proposal in person.

11. If you plan to mail your proposal, write a short cover letter to go with it.

A PROPOSAL FOR A HIKING CLUB
PRESENTED TO THE FACULTY
AT NORTHWEST JUNIOR HIGH
Sept. 11, 1989

We, the students of Room 115, want to organize a hiking club for the eighth grade. The club will meet on the last Friday of every month and will plan three hikes during the year. A bus will drive the students to the hiking area.

Plan
1. Miss Tolman will be the faculty sponsor.
2. A survey of the students proved there are many who are interested.
3. We could meet in Miss Tolman's room to plan the hikes.
4. Miss Tolman knows a professional climber who will train everyone.

Needs
1. Climbing equipment.
2. Bus to drive students to climbing areas and to return students to school.

Budget
1. One bus - at $40.00 rental (3 times)............$120.00
2. Equipment per student (used).................$ 50.00
3. The money will be raised at a white elephant sale to be held the second Friday of October after school.

Laurie Baker

Minatare, Nebraska. In Minatare, it had become "cool" for parents to throw keg parties for their high school children on prom night. Laurie Baker grew concerned for her classmates who were drinking and driving.

"Kids were getting really careless. Being in 4-H and Campfire Girls gave me a strong background to have courage to support my beliefs," she says.

Laurie attacked the problem head-on with a proposal for an alcohol-free Safe Prom Night party. She took her proposal to the principal, the school board, and the student council. School officials refused to accept her proposal, and the students didn't act too enthusiastic about it either. So Laurie launched out on her own. Turning to the community, she proposed her idea to the American Legion, who agreed to host the prom at their post.

Surprisingly, kids flocked to the party, and the first Safe Prom Night was a hit. It was repeated the following year, and since then has become a tradition, passed on by Laurie to younger classmates. ◉

Laurie and her escort at the Safe Prom Night dance.

POWER FUNDRAISING

Fundraising can be fun. And if you can put money where your mouth is—if you can solve your problem or support your project with dollars you donate—this can sometimes persuade officials to act on your ideas.

Fundraising can also be a good learning experience. Handling money gives you a hands-on chance to collect sizable sums and keep track of them. Just remember these two important tips:

▶ Save the money you collect in a safe place, such as a bank.

▶ Make sure that at least two people stay with the money at all times until it's deposited.

Kids have successfully raised money in many ways. Here are some suggestions for you to try.

Six Ways to Fundraise

1. HOLD A WHITE ELEPHANT SALE. Schools or groups can raise amazing amounts of money by selling seemingly useless objects. Besides, parents will appreciate it if you and your friends strip your bedrooms of all the wheelless cars and abandoned Barbie dolls. Sell everything you collect for fifty cents to a dollar, if you can.

Highland Park School in Salt Lake City, Utah, raised almost $1,500 in a white elephant sale, simply by selling used stuff from home. It's a lot of work, but every dollar you bring in is pure profit.

> **YOU ONLY TRIUMPH WHEN YOU ADD THE "UMPH" TO "TRY"**

2. SELL COMMERCIALLY PREPARED FOOD. Raise dough by pitching pizzas, popcorn, or candy bars. Food producers or businesses will sometimes donate these items, if you give them free advertising in return.

Would you rather sell homemade goodies? Check first to see if your state requires you to have a food handler's license.

3. SELL SERVICES. Hold fairs, dances, talent shows, auctions, film showings, tours, and so on. If you don't mind getting wet, there are always car washes.

4. ASK FOR DONATIONS. Your school or community may give you money to raise money. For example, a service organization may pay your mailing costs for sending a fundraising letter. You'll find as example of a fundraising letter on the next page.

5. CAMPAIGN. In some states, it's legal during election times to get paid to campaign for officials who are running for office. Jackson kids have raised money in this way. However, this activity should probably *not* be connected with a school, and probably should be supervised by parents.

6. ASK FOR IN-KIND DONATIONS. Businesses may donate time and materials to help you with your problem or project. Employees may be willing to work with you. Printers may agree to print letters or leaflets for free.

You can probably brainstorm many more creative ways to raise money. So go for it!

 **Salt Lake City School District**

Jackson Elementary School
750 West 200 North
Salt Lake City, Utah 84116
March 14, 1988

_____
_____
_____
_____

To Whom It May Concern:

Thanks for our many pledges. Our bill has passed the legislature, and the governor has signed it. It is now a law. The law sets up a State Contributory Superfund to help clean up hazardous waste. It is now a legal fund.

We would like to thank you very much for your support. You may now send in your pledge in the amount of _____ to the following address:

Jackson Contributory Superfund
c/o Salt Lake Education Foundation
440 East First South
Salt Lake City, Utah 84111

Thank you again.

Sincerely,

Christina Lingbloom
Lauren Evans

Lauren Evans,
Christine Lingbloom, and

All Children in the
Extended Learning Program

Grants: Where the Big Bucks Are

Another way to raise funds is by getting a grant. (A *grant* is a sum of money that is given to a person or group for a specific purpose.) To get a grant, you first have to know where to look. Government agencies, corporations, and foundations are all good sources of grant money. Second, you have to apply for grants. Making out applications can be complicated and time-consuming, but very worthwhile if you receive the money you request.

Even after you get a grant, your work may not be finished. Special grants called *matching grants* require you to "match" all or part of the grant with money you raise in other ways. For example, let's say your group applies for a $1,000 grant to make needed repairs in a neighborhood park. You win the grant—but to get it, you have to raise $300 on your own. (This would be a 30 percent match.) So you hold a white elephant sale at the park building.

If you're willing to make the effort to find and apply for grants, the rewards can be big bucks—hundreds, even thousands of dollars to fund your idea.

GOVERNMENT GRANTS

Jackson children have applied for four grants and received two. The two they received were neighborhood development grants for $1,800 each, which the children used to plant trees. To raise the $360 required to match each grant, the kids sold popcorn and pizzas. They found tree nurseries that agreed to donate a few trees. They asked the local power company to help by digging holes with an auger for the 400-pound baby red maples. And they sought assistance from the urban forester, who used his tractor to lift the trees into the ground.

Grant money is available through many federal and state agencies. It's worth going after, especially if you need large sums. You might be surprised at how much money is available, if you can find it.

Most states, cities, and towns also have grants available. You just have to get out your Sherlock Holmes magnifying glass and go snooping.

Officials aren't used to receiving requests for grant money from kids. For that reason, you'll probably get their attention more easily than an adult group.

A BOOK WITH INFORMATION ABOUT GOVERNMENT GRANTS

Look for this book at your library reference desk:

☞ The *Catalogue of Federal Domestic Assistance* (U.S. Government Printing Office, published annually). Describes federal programs and services which provide assistance or benefits to American people. Lists sources of federal grant money by agencies, tells how to apply, gives regulations, etc.

UTAH NEEDS 2,000,000 TREES!

One tree will clean up $62,000 of air pollution in a 50 year lifetime!
Join the "Leaf it to Us - Children's Crusade for trees"!

Would your school like matching money for planting trees on public property?

Money available on a First-come, First-serve basis.

(Grants from: National Assn. of State Foresters, American Forestry Assn., Utah State Legislature)

HOW To get a grant:

1. Call or write Jackson Elementary, 533-3032, 750 West 200 North, S.L.C., Ut. 84116, to let us know you are interested
   * Do not spend money until you get an answer from us.
2. Choose kinds of trees. Call nurseries to find out prices. Some will donate trees.
3. Decide where to plant. Ask city or County officials where to plant. It must be on public lands.
4. Raise money for your half of the grant.
5. Order trees from Nursery. Send copy of bill To Jackson Elementary. Dick Klason, State Forester, will pay half from the fund. You pay the other half.
6. Plant your trees. Have fun.

(detach)

Name of school _____ contact person _____

address _____ grade _____

telephone # of school _____ home phone - contact _____

Amount of money you want from us _____. Total amount _____. You pay half_____.

Approximate # of trees you plan to plant _____.

Planting location _____.

Kinds of trees _____.

Mail to: Jackson Elementary EXTENDED LEARNING PROGRAM, Rm. 30
          750 West 200 North
          Salt Lake City, Utah 84116

GRANTS FROM CORPORATIONS

Kids Against Pollution (KAP) in Closter, New Jersey, needed help implementing their national information campaign. They received an award grant of $85,000 worth of IBM computer equipment, sponsored by IBM and *U.S. News & World Report.* (To learn more about KAP, see pages 122–125.)

Many corporations can donate up to ten percent of their taxable income to charitable organizations. That means you. And if you're asking, "How can I find out who the corporations are?", you've already taken the first step.

1. Call your chamber of commerce and ask for a pamphlet listing the major corporations in your state. Many state chambers publish these.

2. If yours doesn't, call or visit your city library. Ask at the reference desk where you can find a list of major corporations in your city or state.

3. Call your mayor, city, or county offices. They will often know about special grants you could get to help with a project. Special committees may have money, too—arts councils, city beautification committees, and so on.

It's crazy, but a great deal of money available to communities for improvements is sometimes not used.

BOOKS WITH INFORMATION ABOUT GRANTS FROM CORPORATIONS

Look for these books at your library reference desk. They will tell you a lot about leading corporations. You could try contacting one or more. Ask if they would be willing to sponsor your group with a grant of money.

☞ *Million Dollar Directory: America's Leading Public and Private Companies* (Dun & Bradstreet, 1992). A directory of 160,000 leading companies. Gives addresses, phone numbers, annual sales, contacts, etc.

☞ *Taft Corporate Giving Directory: Comprehensive Profiles of America's Major Corporate Foundations and Corporate Charitable Giving Programs* (The Taft Group, 1992). Listed by subject. Examples: arts, civic and public affairs, education, health, etc. Tells who to contact, plus how and when to apply. This easy-to-use book walks you through the process for each corporation.

Some non-profit organizations also give grants. Look for this book at your library reference desk:

☞ *National Directory of Non-Profit Organizations* (The Taft Group, 1992). An index of groups according to subject: civil rights, schools, housing, farming, etc.

PRIVATE FOUNDATIONS

A *foundation* is an institution that uses private wealth for the public good. You may have heard of some foundations: the Ford Foundation, the Carnegie Foundation, the Rockefeller Foundation, the Lilly Endowment. All were started by very wealthy people who wanted to use their money to benefit society. In other words, the whole reason foundations exist is to give away money!

As you find out more about foundation grants, you'll probably be amazed at how much money is out there, just waiting for someone to apply.

COMMUNITY FOUNDATIONS

Community foundations are similar to private foundations, except they exist to benefit individual communities. To find out what your area has to offer, pick up the phone or head for your library.

1. Contact your chamber of commerce. Ask if they publish directories of major clubs and associations in your state. They should at least be able to tell you which groups to contact, like the Kiwanis, Lions, or other service clubs. Some chambers have money of their own available for worthwhile projects.

2. The Foundation Center's regional collections (city libraries) might also have information on community sources of grant money.

BOOKS WITH INFORMATION ABOUT FOUNDATION GRANTS

Look for these books at your library reference desk:

☞ *The Foundation Grants Index* (The Foundation Center, 1991). Lists grants by state. The Foundation Center also publishes volumes of grants according to subject—for example, family services, community and urban development, elementary and secondary education, science, recreation, etc. Ask about any rules they may have for people or groups who apply for grants.

☞ *Grants for Children and Youth* (The Foundation Center, 1992). Describes grants to nonprofit organizations in the U.S. and abroad for youth-related activities. Examples: service programs, education, health, medical care, programs for parents and teachers. Lists national foundations and how to contact them.

☞ *National Data Book of Foundations: A Comprehensive Guide to Grantmaking Foundations* (The Foundation Center, 1992). Lists independent, company-sponsored, and community foundations by state.

The Foundation Center also has regional collections where you can find lists of foundations and the amounts of money they grant to different groups. Many of the regional collections publish an annual report.

Most major city libraries function as regional collections. You don't even have to go there in person—you can usually call on the phone and request the information you need.

How to Write a Winning Grant Application

You've discovered a grant you want to apply for. Before you ask for a grant application, you need to find out if kids are eligible for that particular grant.

If your project is school-related, you may need district permission to apply for a grant. And you'll want to know if there are any restrictions on how you can spend the grant money, if you get it. For example, if what you want to do is repair your park, it doesn't make sense to apply for a grant that can only be used to buy library books.

Does the grant specify matching money? If it says that you must raise twenty cents for every dollar of grant money, can you do it?

How fast do you need the money? Federal grants usually require a six- to eight-month waiting period between the time they award a grant and the time they make the money available. If a federal grant is in your future, be sure to plan ahead.

And make sure that you've thoroughly researched your problem before applying for a grant. You'll need to explain your case clearly, positively, and in detail. Many more people and groups may be applying for the same grant. You must convince the granting organization that your project is the most worthy one.

When you're ready to apply for your grant, use the grant application checklist on page 164 to organize your information before you fill out the application.

IMPORTANT
• • • • • • • • •
Keep copies and records of EVERYTHING you do to apply for your grant and achieve your goals. Keep track of when and how you spend the grant money. The more records you have—and the more complete they are—the better.

Raton Future Farmers of America

Raton, New Mexico. In a rough, mountainous area of New Mexico, there exists an inspiring Future Farmers of America (FFA) leader named Ray Chelewski. Ray believes that hard work builds character in kids, and that leadership prepares them for the future. He and his group of 80 gutsy teenagers received a contract from their state to spearhead the reclamation project for Sugarite State Park.

"People here had never done anything like this project," explains Bob Salter, an official with the mining and minerals division of the New Mexico natural resources department. "The work [done by the FFA kids] was better than we often get from professional contractors."

In the 1900's, Sugarite had been mined for coal. The tailings (mining wastes) had been dumped nearby. Over the years, the tailings had begun to erode, polluting streams and endangering tourists.

To reclaim the area, the Raton chapter dug 1,074 seed basins, built 51 rock check dams, terraced 781 feet of steep slopes, and built a diversion channel to change the flow of a small stream. They cleaned a 4 1/2 mile trail in the park and made 150 markers for the trail. They welded 65 metal frame picnic tables in a shop class and set them up throughout the park.

For their services, each student received $1,000. But their benefits went beyond money. As Remy Martinez says, "It was hot. It was hard work, and we got really dirty. But everybody helped everybody else out, and we got it done."

And that's not all they did. The Future Farmers planted an experimental tree farm and installed drip irrigation. Then they constructed and operated a facility to care for injured and orphaned wild game.

Elizabeth Morgan adds, "I gained leadership skills I was lacking. I have become comfortable with public speaking and have lost my shyness with my classmates." In a project like the Sugarite reclamation, Elizabeth points out, "students build themselves as well as their communities." ◉

Tim Barraclough, Jr., Raton FFA Chapter, helps Clyde the black bear at the facility to care for injured and orphaned wild game.

Courtesy Betta Ferrendelli, *Raton Range Newspaper*

POWER MEDIA COVERAGE AND ADVERTISING

> ## " In the future, everyone will be famous for 15 minutes. "
>
> *Andy Warhol*

Wouldn't it be thrilling to see yourself in the newspaper or on TV? It could happen to you. And there's a way to make it happen: Plan an event, then put out the word!

Believe it or not, radio, TV, newspapers, and magazines don't have crystal balls where they can see everything that's going on in a city. They rely on news tips from the public. That means you. And here's more good news: Reporters love to cover stories of kid action.

When reporters show up at your school or project site, hefting their heavy cameras and equipment, it adds an air of excitement and suspense. More than anyone, reporters can create public awareness of your project. You might receive some well-deserved pats on the back. And you'll attract more people who want to join your team.

Never apologize for seeking publicity, and never act embarrassed when reporters respond. That's their job. Reporters want good stories. If your project will benefit your community, everyone should know about it.

So let the media spread your message. Here are some tips to get you started.

66

Attention-Getting Tips

1. Look up radio stations, TV stations, newspapers, and magazines in the yellow pages of your telephone book. Make a list of their addresses and phone numbers.

2. If you're going to be contacting media people on your own, there are two ways to do it. You can call them on the phone and hope they will talk to you. Or you can take a more professional approach and send out news releases. (A *news release*, or *press release*, is a written statement describing an event that is sent out to members of the media.)

If your project is school-related, an employee in the district office may be assigned to write news releases for you. This employee might be called a "public information specialist." Give him the information you collect, and keep him up-to-date on your project.

Reporters may be more interested in news releases written by kids than ones written by adults (even public information specialists).

BOOKS THAT TELL ABOUT THE MEDIA

Look for these books at your library reference desk:

☞ *Broadcasting/Cable Year Book* (Broadcasting Publications, Inc., published annually). A directory of TV and radio stations, with addresses and phone numbers, by state and city.

☞ *Gale Directory of Publications and Broadcast Media* (Gale Research, published annually). Lists newspapers, TV and radio stations, magazines, journals, and other publications in the U.S. by state.

☞ *If You Want Air Time* by Jane Freundel Levey (National Association of Broadcasters, 1987). This easy-to-read booklet tells you how to work with the media. It costs about $3.00. If you would like a copy, write to: Services Department of National Association of Broadcasters, 1771 N Street, N.W., Washington, D.C. 20036. They will mail you an order form.

☞ *The Standard Periodical Directory* (Gale Research, published annually). Lists newspapers, TV and radio stations, magazines, journals, and other publications in the U.S. by state.

DAILY NEWS
MAN BITES CANINE
DOG DIDN'T KNOW WHAT BIT HIM *see pg2*

❝ When a dog bites a man, that is not news, because it happens so often. But if a man bites a dog, that is news. ❞

John B. Bogart

How to Write a News Release

1. Give media people plenty of advance notice of your event. They should receive your release at least two to three weeks ahead of time so they can put you on their calendars. Mail a copy of your release to each reporter on your list.

2. The top of your news release should give the name of the main contact person (that might be you), a telephone number where the reporter can call to find out more, and the date of the news release.

IMPORTANT
• • • • • • • • •

Inform adult supervisors (your principal, teacher, scout leader, parent) about the event you're planning.

Tell them that you're seeking media coverage.

---

3. The body of your news release should answer these questions: *who, what, when, where,* and *why*—the five W's. (On some news releases, the "why" part is included in a paragraph labeled "details.") Keep your statements brief, factual, and clear. Study the example on the next page.

4. Try to come up with a "hook"—something to snag reporters' attention without giving away your whole story. If it's appropriate, use a little humor. It will make your release more memorable.

5. If you're going to act professional by sending a news release, then your release should look professional, too. It's a good idea to type it or write it on a computer. Double-space, and keep it to one short page if at all possible. You can also write it by hand, as long as it's readable.

If you absolutely can't survive without two pages, type the word "more" at the bottom of the first page, and type "-30-" at the end of the release. ("-30-" is a code that means "the end.")

Copy and use the news release form on page 165 to organize your information before you prepare the final copy of your news release.

Jackson kids plant eighteen 400-pound red maple trees near their school.

Courtesy Paul Barker, *Deseret News*

NEWS RELEASE

FOR IMMEDIATE RELEASE   Contact: Barbara Lewis, Teacher
                                                 Jackson Elementary
                                                 (801) 533-3032

April 10, 1989

WHAT: Jackson School children will plant 18 red maple trees on
               Eighth West on April 20th to 21st.

Who: Nine sixth-grade children in the Extended Learning
               Program (for academically talented) originated,
               researched, and carried out the entire project.

When: April 20-21, 1989. The project will commence at 10:00
               a.m. on April 20th with an opening ceremony in which the
               children will explain their project. Mayor Palmer
               DePaulis is planning to deliver a short speech. The
               planting will continue until 3:00 p.m.

               Planting will continue April 21st from 9:00 to 3:00 p.m.

Where: Beginning at Eighth West and Third North, it will
               continue down to Second South.

Details: The children raised $2,400 to finance the project
               through applying for and receiving a city grant, through
               weekly popcorn sales, and through the donation of two
               trees by Native Plants, Inc. The children solicited
               help from U.P.& L. to dig holes with an auger for the
               children's 400-pound baby trees. The children have
               dubbed the red maples with such unique names as "Lady
               Di," "JFK," and "Dog's Re-Leaf."

What to Do After You Send Your Release— and When the Reporters Arrive

1. Once you've sent your release, telephone media people a few days before your event to remind them.

2. Although reporters don't like "canned" answers, practice ahead of time how you might answer questions like: What is your project? Why do you want to do it? What have you learned? How did you become interested in it?

If you practice, you won't find your tongue getting caught between your teeth when you're interviewed.

3. It's natural to feel nervous about talking to reporters. Practice relaxing, too. And remember: It won't really matter if you stumble while you're talking. Anything filmed by TV camera crews is edited before it's aired, and newspapers don't print stutters and mumbles.

4. Prepare a one-page outline describing your project—what you've done, what you're planning to do—and make copies to give to each reporter. This simplified press kit will help to ensure that reporters tell your story like it is. (A *press kit* is a packet of information—background facts, photographs, and so on—that is prepared especially for reporters. Press kits are often given out before press conferences.)

5. Provide enough space for reporters, photographers, and their equipment. Reserve a place for them to stand or sit where they can see and hear what's going on.

6. Write down the names of the reporters who cover your event. When you plan another activity, call the same people on the phone and tell them about it. They will remember you.

7. When your event is over, write and send thank-you notes to all the reporters who came. This is polite to do—and the reporters will love it.

8. What if reporters don't show up? Even if they told you they wanted to? Remember that reporters must cover many events, planned and unplanned. If someone robs a bank at the same time, they'll probably zip over there instead. Hold your event anyway.

More Ways to Advertise

News releases are just the tip of the iceberg when it comes to getting attention. Read about these other ways to advertise your project or event, then brainstorm more of your own.

1. COMMUNITY CALENDARS. Many neighborhoods and cities maintain community calendars of coming events. If you advertise here, you will reach an audience of officials, as well as the public.

Check deadlines for entries. Write a few concise statements (who, what, where, when, and why) and give the name and phone number of a contact person.

2. NEWSLETTERS. Clubs, churches, and other organizations often send out newsletters. Why not advertise in these?

3. PERSONAL INTERVIEWS AND TALK SHOWS. Did you know that TV and radio stations often allow free time for public comments? Call or write your local stations to ask for time to discuss your project on the air.

Many cable TV stations must set aside blocks of time for community access. Maybe you can have your own show! The "Tree Musketeers" did. Read about them on page 75.

4. PRESS CONFERENCES. A *press conference* is a meeting all media people are invited to attend. It usually lasts about 30 minutes, and includes a question-and-answer period for reporters.

You should not try this unless you have a really good reason—for example, an important dignitary who will be addressing a vital issue.

If you do have a really good reason, announce your press conference with a news release. For tips on writing a news release, see page 68.

5. FLYERS. Flyers are a fairly simple way to tell a great many people about your event. To get them out, you can use the mail or muscle power (in other words, hand-delivery).

Your flyer should be one page or less and should answer (you guessed it) the usual questions: who, what, when, where, and why. Also include a statement which gives people a reason to attend. What's in it for them?

Make your flyer interesting to look at and to read. Include a strong statistic, an anecdote, or a few fascinating facts. Use large lettering for the headlines. If appropriate, illustrate your flyer. Humor will grab your readers' attention.

You'll find an example of a flyer on the next page.

PSA's with Punch

The PSA (Public Service Announcement) is a short statement which advertises an event or expresses concern for a problem. Most radio and television stations also offer free air time for PSA's.

A PSA is more formal than a personal interview or a talk show. Community groups are usually allowed specific time slots—10 seconds, 20 seconds, 30 seconds, 60 seconds, and sometimes more—to get their message across, so you must plan carefully. (Thirty seconds is a lot longer than you may think.) Since there is a great deal of competition for these time slots, you must have a project which will affect a large audience.

To create a strong PSA, you'll probably need help from professionals—sound experts and/or camera people. Contact individual stations for guidelines on length, content, and eligibility.

Sometimes stations will write a PSA for you. Write and ask them. You'll find a sample letter on page 73.

How to Write a PSA

Before you do anything else, contact your local TV and radio stations to find out if they have any special rules for PSA's. For example, will your PSA have to be a certain number of seconds long?

Copy and use the PSA form on page 166, or create a form of your own. Remember to answer the five W's: who, what, when, where, and why. Check out the example on page 74.

1. Write the name and address of your group at the top.

2. Briefly describe your *target audience* (the people you want to reach with your message).

3. Tell when your PSA should *begin* and *end* running on the air.

4. List a contact person (you?) and a phone number (yours?) the station can call to get more information.

5. Briefly state your topic (what your PSA is about).

6. Write the text. You could include two versions: a short one (maybe 10 seconds) and a longer one (maybe 30 seconds). This will give the station a choice.

7. Time your PSA while reading it aloud. Tell how many seconds it lasts.

8. Write "-*end*-" at the bottom. This means that the text of the PSA is finished.

H.B. 154- Leaf it to us Childrens Crusade For Trees

U.S. NEEDS 100,000,000 trees -
Utah needs 2,000,000 trees -

The Problem:

1. Tropical rain forests the size of Tennessee are being burned every year.
2. The build up of CO_2 has grown, causing world warm up (Green House Effect).
3. The U.S. has 1/20 of world Pop., but produces 1/4 of the CO_2.
4. For every 4 trees that die in U.S. cities, only one is planted.

WHAT TREES CAN DO TO HELP:

1. One tree in a 50 year life time will:
   (a) Clean up $62,000 dollars worth of air pollution.
   (b) Give off $31,250 of oxygen.
   (c) Recycle $37,000 worth of water.
   (d) Prevent $31,250 worth of soil erosion.
2. Trees can absorb carbon dioxide at the rate of 48 pounds per year - about 10 tons per acre per year.
3. Trees help save energy. Three trees around your house can cut your air conditioning bill 10-50%.

WHAT H.B. 154 CAN Do:

1. Make a fund for $10,00 for children (K-12) to plant trees across the state on public lands.
2. Money would be kept in the state forestry funds.
3. Kids would apply for grants and match the money.
4. We will double your money.

Please support H.B. 154

Information from: American Forestry Association, & University of Michigan, Forestry Update.

 **Salt Lake City School District**

Jackson Elementary School
750 West 200 North
Salt Lake City, Utah 84116
April 18, 1988

KISN
P.O. Box 16028
S.L.C., Utah 84116
Attention: Shelli

Shelli,

Jackson Elementary called in late November to announce our Christmas Sale for donations to help clean up hazardous waste. Thank you for the announcement.

Now the Future Problem Solving team has won the National Community Problem Solving Contest. We have been invited to go to the University of Michigan to accept a national award. We have to raise the money to go ourselves. Would you make an announcement on the radio like you did before with this information? We will need the money by the middle of May. We have to raise about $2,500.00. Thank you again.

Sincerely,

Heather Hilliard

Heather D. Hilliard
Sixth grade student
Jackson Elementary

P.S. This award is for our hazardous waste project.

PUBLIC SERVICE ANNOUNCEMENT

JACKSON ELEMENTARY SCHOOL
750 West Second South
Salt Lake City, Utah 84109

TARGET AUDIENCE: youth groups, adult advisors
BEGINNING DATE: Sept. 1, 1990   ENDING DATE: Oct. 1, 1990
CONTACT PERSON: Donald Seher   PHONE: 555-2022

MONEY FOR KIDS TO PLANT TREES

<u>30 seconds</u>   Plant a tree today to save our future. Trees
save more than money. They can save our envi-
<u>63 words</u>   ronment. Trees recycle water and prevent soil
erosion. One tree in its average 50-year
lifetime will provide $62,000 worth of air
pollution control.
One tree.

Matching grants of money are available to
school children throughout Utah to plant
trees. For more information, call 467-HERB.

— end —

(Written by Donald Seher, sixth grade, Jackson Elementary)

74

El Segundo Scouts

El Segundo, California. What do thirteen eight-year-olds do on a spring day in a sunny state? They skate, trade Barbie doll clothes, and slurp icy drinks, right? Wrong. At least one troop of Scouts sits down under a tree and plans how they can save the ozone layer.

As ten-year-old Sabrina Alimahomed tells it, "I'd rather be helping our environment, because if people don't do anything, the hole in the ozone will keep getting bigger, and we'll dig holes and live underground."

A group called "Tree Musketeers" was born under that tree, and it has since branched out to include hundreds of other scout troops and people from the community. These ambitious young people and their inspiring leaders, Gail Church and Kathy Barrett, created a public awareness campaign to inform others about the value of trees. They hosted El Segundo's First Annual Arbor Day Celebration and have planted hundreds of trees in their area.

But their most creative way to reach the public was to write, perform, and produce a half-hour TV game show called "Tree Stumpers" to educate school kids on the importance of trees.

"Tree Stumpers" was aired on TV on a community cable station and has been repeated several times. Parts of the "Tree Stumpers" show have been "snipped out" and used by the cable people as PSA's for the environment.

To sink their roots down even deeper, Tree Musketeers has incorporated and is now recognized as a genuine non-profit group. Not only will this make the group more respected, it will also make it easier for them to raise money. (Read more about incorporating on pages 89–90.)

As sponsor Gail Church put it, "The only holes we plan to dig are those in which trees live." ◉

Tree Musketeers write, produce, and direct their own TV game show, "Tree Stumpers."

On the set of the "Tree Stumpers" show.

Courtesy Gail Church

Audrey Chase

Remember Audrey Chase? The Jackson Elementary kid who passed a petition at the United Nations and flew to Washington, D.C., to lobby for money for kids across the nation to plant trees? You read about her on page 11.

Audrey tackled another great project. She wrote and appeared in a four-minute Arbor Day TV news story about the importance of trees. Audrey was contacted by Dave Block, a reporter from one of the three major TV stations in Salt Lake City. She wrote the script while sitting in the TV station studio, legs swinging beneath a swivel chair. Dave Block helped her put her script in the correct form. Audrey chose the people to interview and narrated the story herself.

**KSL-TV NEWSCAST
WRITTEN BY AUDREY CHASE
Age 10, Jackson Elementary
Salt Lake City, Utah**

Audrey Chase "up a tree" at the beginning of her newscast.

AUDREY'S TREES

Hi, my name is Audrey Chase. I'm here to tell you that trees are my buddies. Trees are beautiful, fun to climb, and give us shade to cool us off in the summer.

They are also good for building tree houses. A tree can also be a home for animals, and some trees give us food to eat.

But trees are not just for fun. They also help the environment. Did you know that one tree in its 50-year average lifetime can contribute $62,000 worth of air pollution control?

Trees are important to me so we can save our environment and live a more healthy life.

(Audrey hops out of tree.)

Audrey interviews Aaron Webster.

Audrey interviews Thelma and Burt Schauguaard.

Photos courtesy Barbara Lewis

One tree can recycle water, provide oxygen for us, and control soil erosion at a savings of almost $100,000...and that's a lot of money!

In my class at school we started learning about the importance of trees. I realized that if we didn't have trees, we couldn't live. I started looking for places that I could plant trees. I didn't want any open spaces, unless it was for flying kites or playing ball.

This is my front yard. Here is the first tree I planted. It's a honey locust. Since then, I planted ten more near the Children's Museum. I named these two trees. This one is named after Dick Klason, a State Forester...and a big help. This one is named Ted E. Bear Lewis...he is a member of the State House of Representatives. He helped us to get money from the legislature for more trees.

This is my friend, Aaron Webster. He thinks trees are important, too.

(Audrey interviews Aaron about why he values trees.)

Some other friends of mine, Burt and Thelma Schauguaard, think trees are so important they paid a lot of money to move their trees from their old house to their new house.

(Audrey interviews Schauguaards about why they care for trees.)

I think trees are so important I wrote a letter to President Bush asking him to set aside money so kids can plant trees across the nation.

(Audrey is interviewed live by TV Reporter at Warm Springs Park with classmates. They end by planting a tree together.) ◉

POWER PROCLAMATIONS

You probably think that mayors and governors are the only ones who can write proclamations. Not true! You can write one, too. It's easy.

A proclamation is just a fancy way of making an announcement to the public. It can also be used to recognize someone who has made an important contribution of some kind. Proclamations are usually made by officials, but there are no punishments awaiting inventive kids who write one themselves. You might like to recognize someone who has been helpful to your cause.

Mayors are usually willing to make proclamations on your behalf. For example, suppose you want to advertise an anti-drug campaign. You could kick it off by asking your mayor to proclaim a certain week as "Kick Out Drugs Week."

Councils or commissions might also write proclamations or resolutions in much the same way. When a governor writes one, it might be called a *declaration*. Since "proclamation," "resolution," and "declaration" are often general terms, any official can create one on his or her official stationery.

In the past, mayors and commissions across the nation have written proclamations for many different kinds of causes, including:

► Environmental Awareness Month
► Bike to Work Week
► Kindness to Animals Week
► Youth of America Week
► Bill Superfoot Wallace Day
► Shake Off the Flab Week
► Minority Business Development Week
► Chew the Fat With a New Friend Day

What would you like to proclaim? Use your imagination!

Proclamation Tips

1. Copy and use the proclamation form on page 167 to make yours look official. To get an idea of what to say and how to say it, study the example on page 81.

2. Contact your mayor's office at least a month in advance to request the proclamation. The mayor's secretary can set up a time and place for you to meet. You should also send a letter stating exactly what you would like the mayor to write.

3. When you arrive (preferably at the mayor's office) for your appointment, the mayor will probably have your proclamation ready. Usually, a mayor will allow you to take a photograph with him or her signing the proclamation. This photo can be used for advertising your project, if you get the mayor's permission first.

Jackson kids receive a proclamation from Salt Lake City Mayor Palmer DePaulis.

Barbara Lewis

Hawthorne Elementary

Salt Lake City, Utah. "Wait! Don't toss out that newspaper! Save that aluminum can!" The fourth, fifth, and sixth graders at Hawthorne Elementary in Salt Lake City, Utah, are serious about recycling. If one of these energetic kids can corner you, he or she will wring a promise out of you to save all your toilet paper tubes and old clothes hangers in order to make a super marble shoot for their "Recycled Invention Fair." Or Eric, Ernie, or McKay will sidle up to sell you their triangular shaped earrings made out of old cans. Only $2.00 a pair. What a bargain!

But their teacher, Sheri Sohm, encouraged them to think bigger. So the kids carried their recycling idea to the community, collecting 15,000 cans at their school and starting the Sugarhouse Recycling Center for Newspapers. And some of the children have even served on the mayor's recycling committee.

They call themselves "KOPE"—Kids Organized to Protect the Environment. They have planted a garden in their school yard, written and presented plays, organized their own Earth Day art fair, and written a newsletter. They have started KOPE groups in other schools and hosted two intra-district meetings with 15 other schools to encourage projects to celebrate Earth Week. ☉

Hawthorne Elementary kids open a recycling center in Salt Lake City, Utah.

Courtesy Jeff Allred and Will Fehr, *Salt Lake Tribune*

Salt Lake City Mayor Palmer DePaulis even made a proclamation in their behalf. Here is what it said:

Proclamation

WHEREAS, one of the most important issues facing the world is the protection of our environment, and

WHEREAS, we need to do all we can to help keep our environment clean, from recycling paper and cans to planting trees, and

WHEREAS, we must help increase public awareness of environmental issues, and

WHEREAS, the Hawthorne Elementary sixth grade has initiated "We Need a Neat Environment Day" as a way to remind people of the importance of helping protect our environment, and

WHEREAS, our community should support the efforts of its citizens to protect our environment, including the campaign brought forth by Hawthorne Elementary students,

NOW, THEREFORE, be it resolved by the Salt Lake City Council and Mayor that we hereby join the sixth grade of Hawthorne Elementary in proclaiming April 17th, 1990 as:

"We Need a Neat Environment Day"

and ask all our citizens to help in whatever way he or she can to keep our community an environmentally safe place in which to live.

SIGNED AND SEALED this 5th day of April, 1990.

PALMER A. DEPAULIS, Mayor

POWER POSITIONS:
GAINING REPRESENTATION ON LOCAL BOARDS AND COUNCILS

Every time your local school board has a meeting, it affects you. Board members might make decisions about what requirements are necessary for graduation, when you have vacations, what you must learn each year, whether to adopt a year-round school, whether to shorten or lengthen the school day, and many more issues that determine what school is like for you.

There are probably hundreds of committee meetings in your community every week. These committees are making decisions that touch your life, including what rules will govern education, recycling and environmental choices, traffic regulations, health standards, and almost anything else you can think of.

But *where are the kids?* Are you sitting on those boards and councils, helping to make those decisions, or are you just accepting whatever they decide? You may not realize it, but you do have a choice.

And how about adult councils in 4-H clubs, Boy Scouts and Girl Scouts, youth leagues and societies, and sports organizations? Have you ever wanted to add something to a program or change a rule? Well, you can.

Jackson kids attended their local community council several times before it dawned on Kory Hansen and April Chacon to ask why kids weren't represented there. They asked for and won permission to sit on the council in an advisory capacity. (To be in an *advi-*

sory capacity means that you can't vote on decisions. But you can offer your opinions and advice.)

During that year, Kory and April helped to make decisions like: (1) what should be done with trains that kept traffic tied up for twenty minutes or more; (2) what to do with abandoned houses; and (3) which streets or buildings needed improvement. Sometimes they thought that being on the council was boring, but they loved the feeling of power they had when making decisions for their neighborhood.

Aaron Iversen and Jamie Atwood, two more Jackson children, sought representation on the PTA board. Kory asked for the opportunity to speak at the general meeting, and got permission for kids to sit with the board as advisors. They helped to make decisions that affected all of the kids in the school.

Serving on PTA boards is something many students do. As another option, you can form a PTSA (Parents, Teachers, Students Association). If you choose to do this, you will probably have to pay dues to the organization, because PTSA's usually require dues from all members.

Children at Hawthorne Elementary in Salt Lake City served on the mayor's recycling committee, making suggestions about recycling aluminum cans and paper.

Do you want to help make important decisions like these? It won't happen unless you ask for the right. If you're interested, here are some tips to try.

Tips for Gaining Representation

1. Find the right agency or council. What kinds of things are you interested in? Follow one of your interests. Call your chamber of commerce or city offices (the mayor, the city council) to ask if there are any committees serving on that subject.

For example:

If you're interested in...	you might try...
animals	the Humane Society
environmental issues	the Sierra Club
	national wildlife groups
health issues	state health agencies
	Red Cross

Most communities have neighborhood councils you could attend. While you're there, ask for more suggestions of groups you might join. Or try your board of education. Why not?

2. Use your social action skills! You could pass a petition, gaining other kids' signatures, to ask for representation on a particular board or council. (Read about petitions on pages 50–53.) Let newspaper and TV reporters know that you're seeking representation. Making the public aware of your idea increases your chances of being accepted. (Find out how to get media coverage on pages 66–77.) You might also write a proposal. (Learn how on pages 54–56.)

3. Be aware that it's more possible for you to sit on a board or council as a student advisor than to become a voting member. But you can have power to influence decisions as an advisor.

4. Meetings might be boring to you. They will be less boring if you assert yourself and *ask questions.* Ask the other members to repeat or explain anything you don't understand. If you get involved in the discussions, meetings will be much more exciting for you. And you never know—you may even teach the committee a thing or two about how to get things done faster. Kids seem to know how to cut through red tape.

5. Don't allow yourself to be put down by anyone. Most people will appreciate your ideas. And most will answer your questions respectfully and explain things to you. You have a right to know what's going on and to understand it.

6. Always be polite, even if you sometimes get discouraged or angry.

" Only those who dare to fail greatly can ever achieve greatly. "

Robert Kennedy

Stanford Pugsley

Salt Lake City, Utah. "Younger and younger kids are becoming more aware of what's going on," says Stanford Pugsley. "They're reading newspapers. Once kids start getting interested and not just worrying about their own lives, they'll get the whole view and make a differ-

ence in the world. But the large majority of the population at my school isn't even close."

Who is Stanford Pugsley? He's the newest member of the Salt Lake City Board of Education. This 16-year-old honor student had the courage to put an obscure Utah law to the test. The 1986 law stated that any student who could collect the signatures of 500 peers could request appointment to the board as a non-voting member. Stan was the first to do it in Salt Lake, and now he's serving a one-year term. ☉

Stanford Pugsley before the Salt Lake City Board of Education, where he serves as student advisor.

Courtesy Garry Bryant, *Deseret News*

POWER CAMPAIGNING

You may not want to be a leader yourself, but it's your responsibility to choose good leaders to follow. And believe it or not, kids can campaign for officials, and they can turn the tide in an election.

The next time an election rolls around, don't just sit back. Get involved! Study the candidates and their issues. Read newspaper reports and watch speeches on TV. Then pick a candidate and find out how you can help.

Campaigning Tips

1. Include your parents in your plans.

2. Call your candidate's campaign office, which will usually be listed in your phone book under the name of the political party. Or call your neighborhood council to learn the location of campaign headquarters. Pick up the phone or walk in the door. Tell them you're ready and willing to volunteer.

3. You might get involved in attending mass meetings, helping with voter registration, handing out flyers, speaking door-to-door, interviewing, surveying neighborhoods, creating and distributing signs and posters, soliciting support from various groups, making telephone calls, and so on. For every political campaign, there are a million different things to do. Use your social action skills!

Kory Hansen

Salt Lake City, Utah. Remember Kory Hansen, who won permission to sit on his local community council? (Find this story on page 82.) The night he went to the meeting to ask why there weren't any kids on the council, the candidates who were running for re-election to the State Legislature were there, too. So Kory (who "turns on" if you put him anywhere near a microphone) gave his speech to council members and candidates.

Kory Hansen

Kory also met the candidates and asked them, "Is there any way you could help us raise some money?" The Jackson kids had just won the President's Youth Environment Award, he explained. They had been invited back to Washington, D.C., to receive the award in person. They needed more money to get there.

Senator Rex Black, who sponsored the kids' hazardous waste bill in the Utah Senate, told Kory that he might be able to help. If the kids were willing to go door-to-door, campaigning for his re-election, the Senator would pay them $300.00 from his campaign funds. (This is legal in Utah if certain requirements are followed.)

Representative Ted Lewis, another Jackson kids sponsor, was also up for re-election. The kids wanted to see their two helpful friends kept in office.

Because it's important in Utah that schools don't support one candidate over another, the kids met in the classroom *after* school (not during school time) to organize the project. Their parents came to the meeting and later traveled with them to each house over about a 40-block area. No one was required to do the campaigning. It was strictly a volunteer project.

Kory, Aaron, Jami, and April divided up the campaign material. Then ten Jackson kids went door-to-door, armed with their most winning smiles. They spoke with residents and left information behind. The people they visited were intrigued with the young campaigners. The kids got blisters from tromping over hard cement for a whole day, but in the evening, they fell on the grass and giggled.

Although one of the political races was a tight one, both Senator Black and Representative Lewis were re-elected. The kids received their $300 and learned that even children can help elect officials of their choice. ◉

POWER VOTER REGISTRATION

> **America is a land where a citizen will cross the ocean to fight for democracy and won't cross the street to vote in a national election.**
>
> *Bill Vaughn*

Did you know that a lot of adults are numb? They're numb from filling out forms, balancing checkbooks, changing diapers, and changing tires. In the pro-cess, many have forgotten the principles our country was founded upon. Many don't think their votes count for anything. They don't even bother to register to vote.

The right to vote belongs to every American citizen of legal age. To exercise that right, people must register in their local *municipalities*—counties or villages. Imagine what could happen if kids attacked their communities in a campaign to shake adults out of the mothballs. Picture what a difference this might make in your neighborhood.

You have the enthusiasm and the energy. You can do it. Along the way, you'll probably become so enthusiastic about the right to vote that you'll never grow into a numb adult yourself.

Know the Rules: Requirements for Registering and Voting

To register to vote, a person:

1. must be a citizen of the United States,
2. must be at least 18 years old by the next election, and
3. must meet the residency requirement.

The residency requirement can get complicated. Call your county or village registration office to get the exact requirement for your area. Try the blue pages in your phone book under "county offices" or "village offices." Or you might find a listing in the white pages under "voting." Or call the League of Women Voters; you'll find their number in the white or yellow pages.

a. A person does *not* have to live in a community for a certain length of time to vote in a federal (national) election—for President, for example, or for a member of congress.

b. Some states *do* have rules for state or local elections. Some states require that a citizen must live within the city, county, or village for up to 30 days before an election in order to vote.

c. Some states allow citizens to register in their *election district* (county or village) during regular office hours a certain number of days before an election. In Arizona, it's 50 days; in Virginia, 31; in all other states, under 30 days.

d. Some states allow citizens to register with deputized agents in their district on certain days before an election. In some states, voters can register at their polling place on the day of an election, as long as they bring valid identification.

TYPES OF ELECTIONS

There are two types of elections: *primary elections*, where voters choose the candidates who will appear on the ballot; and *general elections*, where voters choose the candidates who will actually hold office.

Depending on your state, each election type might have its own registration requirements. For example, to vote in a primary election, a person might need to register as a member of a certain political party, or register several months before the election.

How You Can Help Get Out the Vote

1. You might be able to check out a registration book from your county (or village) clerk's office and carry it door-to-door. With a registration book, you can register voters on the spot.

2. Another way voters can register is with mail-in forms. These are sometimes available at banks, libraries, post offices, or public buildings. You might be able to get mail-in forms from your registration office to deliver door-to-door.

Copy the voter registration form on page 168 for an easy-to-follow script you can use when going door-to-door. Fill out as much of the information as you can ahead of time (part 1, part 2c), then make several photocopies to bring along.

3. You may meet people who say they can't vote or can't register for any number of reasons—they'll be away from home on election day, they're ill, they're dis-

" Bad officials are elected by good citizens who don't vote. "

George Jean Nathan

abled, or they're elderly. Tell them that absentee ballots are available especially for them. The voter will probably have to call or write for a ballot.

4. For many people, English is a second language, and they don't speak it well enough to feel comfortable with registering or voting. Many jurisdictions have *bilingual ballots* available (ballots written in English and another language). See if your election office has some bilingual literature explaining registration and voting. Bring some along on your door-to-door campaign.

5. Kids might be allowed to participate in telephone voter registration campaigns. Check with your registration office or a political party. You might work with a candidate who is running for office by calling to remind people to vote.

6. Use your other social action skills—and your imagination—to get the job done. Write a letter to the editor of your local newspaper, reminding people to vote (see pages 27–28 for letter-writing tips). Pass out your own flyers door-to-door (see page 71). Write a PSA (see pages 71 and 74).

IMPORTANT

Never go door-to-door alone for any reason.

Always get a parent, teacher, or other adult to go with you.

Even if several kids go together in a group, you should ask an adult to accompany you.

POWER ORGANIZING:
INCORPORATING YOUR ORGANIZATION OR GROUP

How would you like to put "Inc." for "Incorporated" after the name of your organization or group? Does that sound impossible or scary? In fact, it's neither. There are a few youth groups around the nation who are incorporating their clubs into mini-businesses.

Tree Musketeers has incorporated. You read about them on page 75. So has Alison Stieglitz (pages 23–24). So has Kids Against Pollution (KAP); you can read about them on pages 122–123.

Why would a group of kids get this fancy? Usually it's because they want to have special status as a *non-profit organization.*

Translated, this means that not only can you identify your group as a specific club, but you also won't have to pay taxes on your club earnings in most cases. And because people who make donations to your group can get a tax deduction for their contributions, you should be able to raise money more easily. Incorporating can give you more credibility.

For example, your club might be financing a huge mailing to kids or groups all over the country. As a result, you have some ongoing expenses. You might even have to pay someone a salary to help out. This is a case when incorporating makes sense.

It's possible, but it isn't easy, so you'll want to get an adult advisor to help. Here are the basic steps you'll need to follow.

How to Incorporate

1. Contact your department of commerce or secretary of state (or comparable office) to file articles of incorporation with your state. You'll have to come up with a name for your group, tell your "duration of operation" (how long you plan to have a club), state your purpose, and so on. You may want to design your own *logo*—a special symbol that stands for your group.

2. Get a business license with your city or county where you'll be doing business. Contact the business licensing division. Tell them what you plan to do, and they'll direct you to the right department.

3. Contact the Internal Revenue Service (IRS) to learn the guidelines for becoming a non-profit organization, and for obtaining a federal I.D. (identification) number.

4. If you want to be classified as a tax-exempt organization, you have to make a special request to the IRS. Then donations to your group will be tax-free.

5. Your advisor can check your *State Code* for specific details. All main libraries have enormous volumes of your *State Code.* Ask your librarian to help you find the one that explains how to incorporate.

If this is the kind of challenge you thrive on, go for it!

Linda Warsaw

San Bernardino, California. At age 12, Linda Warsaw took on a tough project: helping young crime victims.

It all started when Linda and her mother volunteered to help children who had been victims of crimes. While at the district attorney's office, they read through many frightening transcripts of closed cases involving child molestation, kidnappings, and violence.

One day Linda swallowed hard and announced that she would like to attend a real trial. The case involved a

Linda Warsaw

young child who had been molested by a neighborhood baby-sitter. As Linda watched the live courtroom drama unfold, something inside her flipped.

"My stomach turned into a knot," Linda remembers. "I asked myself, 'How can children get victimized like that?' And I decided it was because it was usually with people they knew and trusted. I thought there needed to be a program to educate children to learn how to prevent these crimes. Just because I was a minor and couldn't vote didn't mean I couldn't do anything about the problem."

Linda hustled home and wrote a proposal for "Kids Against Crime" (KAC). Then she showed it to the director of the Victim-Witness Assistance Program, the police, the sheriff, and people at child protective services. Everyone supported the idea, because it was kids fighting for kids.

One year later, in April 1986, KAC was incorporated. It ran on volunteer power for four years before getting funding from city and private foundations to reach its 4,000 members. But kids still run it with their Youth Board of Directors.

Besides teaching crime prevention in schools with skits and fairs, KAC has fingerprinted over 17,000 younger children in the Southern California area. Graffiti-busting members have cleaned their city of unwanted words and scribbles.

A long-awaited dream come true for Linda, KAC even has a hotline for victims or kids who need peer support. The phones are staffed by trained kids, ages 12 to 18, who listen to the problems of the callers and then refer them to professional help.

"A lot of people won't do anything unless they get paid," Linda, now 17, says. "But the reward is just helping other kids and making a safe future."

If you're interested in starting a local chapter or would like more information about KAC, write or call Kids Against Crime, Inc., P.O. Box 22004, San Bernardino, California 92406; telephone (714) 882-1344. ☉

PARADING, PICKETING, AND PROTESTING:
WHEN ALL ELSE FAILS

Have you ever seen crowds of people on the TV news carrying banners or signs, marching down a street or around a public building? Those people are parading, picketing, or protesting. They've reached the end of their rope, and they think that the only way to get attention from public officials is to put on a display of disagreement.

Parading, picketing, and protesting aren't against the law. They're protected by the First Amendment of the United States Constitution—the amendment that provides for freedom of religion, speech, the press, and the right of people "peaceably to assemble." Even kids can parade, picket, and protest, but only as a last resort. These actions are legal as long as they're controlled.

Before planning a "PPP," get permission from your local police department and city offices (mayor or commissioner). Find out about any special regulations you have to follow.

There are many other ways to protest besides parading and picketing. To *boycott* means to refuse to buy or use certain goods or services. Some kids are boycotting fast-food places that use plastic packaging, to protest against the possible hazards to the environment.

Walkouts or *strikes* occur when people leave a meeting, organization, or workplace to show that they disapprove of conditions or rules. Many teachers' unions have held strikes. Teachers have left their classrooms and refused to return until certain changes were made to their contracts or working conditions.

Sit-ins, *sit-downs*, and *demonstrations* are other ways to protest. Protesting is sometimes called *civil disobedience*, because people refuse to follow the established rules.

The main goal of most social protest is to get another organization or group to *compromise*—to meet and settle on differences of opinion. People protest most often when the other side refuses to listen to their concerns.

Because protesting can create disruption in the community, it should never be attempted without serious thought ahead of time. Talk with your parents or other adult advisors before ever trying it.

In other words: Save it for a *really* serious issue.

> **To sin by silence when they should protest makes cowards out of men.**
>
> *Abraham Lincoln*

Youth Force

New York, New York. Picture 25 kids entering drug-infested city parks, organizing basketball games, staging concerts, and offering art instruction to reclaim the parks from crime and drug abusers. Sound incredible? It's happening in midtown Manhattan in New York City.

The idea was born in the heads of kids who protested the drug and prostitution traffic which frightened young people and families away from the parks. Beginning in 1988 with three parks in Manhattan, the program has expanded to include new neighborhoods. The kids, who are known as the Youth Force, are encouraged by the "you-can-do-it" attitude of an adult advisor, Kim McGillicuddy.

The program, called "Take Back the Park," is run by kids for kids. The 15 original staff organizers ranged in age from 12-19 and were considered "high-risk" youth, meaning that some of them had been abused, most were low-income, and the majority came from homes where parents abused alcohol or other drugs. Some of these young organizers lived in apartments. Some lived in hotels. Some were runaways.

The Youth Force invited ten other kids from the Manhattan community to join the planning committee, so the new youth group could be trained to take over the program the following year, when the Force moved on to a new neighborhood. They also invited a few adults from the community, including police and youth group leaders, to join the committee.

After arguing over rules and spending months planning the summer, the Force hit the pavement with flyers and posters to advertise their program. Over 1,200 more kids tagged behind them into the parks instead of hanging out in the streets. The kids supervised the parks. They clapped hands and swung their hips to the rhythmic beat of reggae, salsa, samba, and African music, and enjoyed flicks flashed on the walls of handball courts. They rapped, took part in a youth speakout, went to craft workshops, and filmed a video.

For many, Youth Force was their first job. For others, it was their first success. And for all—kids, parents, neighborhoods, officials—it was proof that kids can make a difference. ☉

Youth Force members advertise their program with flyers and posters

Courtesy Sylvia Pizarro

INITIATING
OR
CHANGING
LAWS

PART THREE

LOCAL LAWS

There's a city ordinance in Salt Lake City, Utah, which makes it illegal to steal a parking space from a car that's already waiting for it. You might have a similar law in your city or town.

If you don't, maybe you should. And maybe you're the one who can do something about it.

Kids doing something about *laws*? Isn't that crazy? Not at all. Local governments tackle such problems as zoning, demolition and replacement of housing, multiple uses of buildings, uses of the downtown area, health issues, public safety, and highway improvements, to name a few. Some of these affect you directly, some indirectly. If you have an idea that could improve the quality of life in your city, why not try to make it legal?

Kids *can* bring about changes at the local level of government. You can do this by using one or more of the social action skills described in Part Two: Power Skills. Or you can try pushing through an actual change in the law.

> **❝ There is nothing permanent except change. ❞**
>
> *Heraclitus*

Learn about Your Local Government

Before you try to change local laws, you should know what kind of government you have. For example, your city may be managed by a mayor and a council, a council and a manager, or a commission. Or it may be run by town meetings, where voters meet to set policies.

You may be learning about your local government in school. If not, maybe you could suggest this as a unit of study, or do a special research project and share the results with your class.

How can you find out what kind of local government you have? Here are some suggestions:

1. Call your local government office and ask them what kind of government they are. Find their number by looking in the blue pages (government section) of your telephone directory.

2. Visit your library reference desk and ask to see *The Municipal Year Book* (International City Management Association, printed annually). This book is a good source of general information about local government.

3. As long as you're at the library anyway, ask if there are other books specifically about your local government.

4. Invite a local official to come to your class and tell you about the government.

BOOKS FOR YOUNG READERS

☞ *First Book of Local Government* by James Eichner (Franklin Watts, 1983). Local government information.

☞ *State and Local Government* by Laurence Santrey (Troll Associates, 1985).

How to Initiate or Change a Local Law

Kids can't actually *make* laws. Only legislative offices can do that. But kids can *initiate* laws—which means that they can have an idea for a law and get the ball rolling. They can have a powerful influence on law-making officials.

You might be surprised at your ability to present problems to officials and convince them to see your side of an issue. (On the other hand, you might change *your* mind after seeing *their* side.)

> **❝ The only man who can change his mind is a man that's got one. ❞**
>
> *Edward Noyes Westcott*

Initiating or changing a law is basically a problem-solving process. This process is described in "Ten Tips for Taking Social Action" on pages 12–13. You may want to review those tips before you begin.

Suppose you pick a problem and research it carefully. The solution you choose is to try to pass a new local law. You have what you think is a good idea for a new law. You gather your evidence—facts, figures, photos, and so on—to make your case. A petition with many signatures can be very powerful (see pages 50–53).

What's next? Here's a brief description of each step and where you come in.

1. CONTACT SOMEONE WHO CAN HELP YOU. When you're ready, contact your local government (mayor, council, commission, administrator, or staff person). You can do this by:
   a. writing a letter (see pages 29–32),
   b. telephoning (see pages 21–23),
   c. making personal contact (for example, arranging for a face-to-face meeting), or
   d. testifying at a meeting (see pages 109–110).

If your problem has a particular location, invite official(s) to go there with you. Jackson kids met their mayor at a park to show him a neglected hill where the lack of vegetation was causing the soil to erode.

2. DISCUSSION. Your proposed law will be discussed by your local lawmaking body. Meanwhile, you should be busy building coalitions of support among people in the community and schools. You should also identify and try to work with your opposition—people who are against what you're trying to do.

3. INVESTIGATION. A staff person will probably decide if there is a need for your proposed law.

4. LEGAL REVIEW. Your proposed law will be investigated to make sure that it doesn't conflict with existing laws.

5. DRAFTING OF YOUR ORDINANCE OR REGULATION. Your proposed law will be officially written in draft (temporary) form, in legal language.

6. PUBLIC DISCUSSION OR HEARING. Your proposed law may be presented in a public meeting for other people to hear about and comment on. *Be sure to be there so you can testify in person.* (For testifying tips, see pages 109–110.)

7. SIGNING, NOT SIGNING, OR VETOING. Your city's chief executive—your mayor, commissioner, or administrator—will do one of three things:
   a. sign your proposed law, making it a real law,
   b. leave it unsigned, or
   c. veto it (reject it).

If the executive leaves your proposed law unsigned, it may become a real law anyway after a certain number of days. This depends on your local government.

STATE LAWS

Creating a law to lower the speed limit in your neighborhood is one thing. But can kids initiate or change *state* laws? You bet they can. YOU can.

Kids at Jackson have started and pushed through two laws in the Utah State Legislature. Other kids have supported or opposed legislation in progress. And it isn't as hard as you might think.

There's a national trend toward giving state legislatures more power. As a result, legislators are working harder to serve their *constituents* (that's you and everyone else living in your district). It's a great time for you to get involved.

> **Most politicians will not stick their necks out unless they sense grass-roots support... Neither you nor I should expect someone else to take our responsibility.**
>
> *Katharine Hepburn*

Learn about Your State Government

State government has three branches:

LEGISLATIVE BRANCH
lawmaking body
(the legislature, house of
delegates, or general court)

EXECUTIVE BRANCH
administrative body
(the governor)

JUDICIAL BRANCH
law-explaining body;
settles disputes (judges, courts)

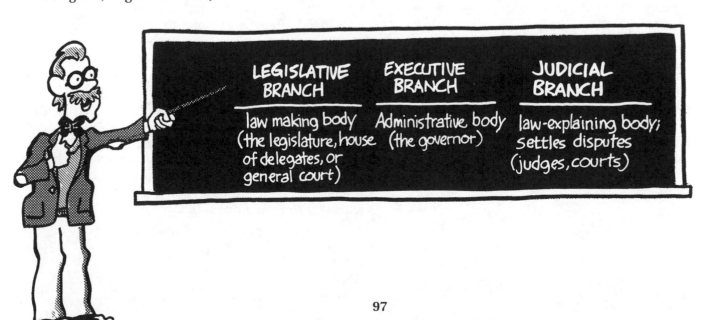

97

Before you try to initiate or change a state law, you should learn as much as you can about your state government. You will feel more comfortable and confident about dealing with officials and lawmakers. And they will be more likely to take you seriously.

Maybe you're already learning about your state government in school. If not, don't let this stop you. Learn on your own.

Look for these books at your library reference desk:

▶ *The Book of States* (The Council of State Governments, printed annually). Information on state government (all three branches), charts, tables, legislative actions, etc.

▶ *BNA's Directory of State Courts, Judges, and Clerks* (The Bureau of National Affairs, 1988). Gives structure and lists of courts by state.

▶ *State Legislative Leadership, Committees, and Staff* (The Council of State Governments, printed annually). Lists state officials by state. If you want to know who in your legislature serves on which committee, you'll find out here.

▶ *State Code.* Each state publishes a separate *State Code* which tells all the laws and rules that pertain to that state. *State Codes* are usually updated every legislative session.

BOOKS FOR YOUNG READERS

☞ *How A Law Is Made: The Story of a Bill Against Air Pollution* by Leonard A. Stevens. (Crowell, 1970). A story of a fictitious bill that becomes a state law.

☞ *States' Rights* by John E. Batchelor (Franklin Watts, 1986). History and development of states' rights.

☞ *State and Local Government* by Laurence Santrey (Troll Associates, 1985).

How to Initiate or Change a State Law

Suppose you have chosen a problem and researched it. You've decided to try to pass a new law, or to change or oppose an existing law. (Take another look at "Ten Tips for Taking Social Action" on pages 12–13.)

You can begin to make or change a state law by contacting someone who can help you. Or, depending on which state you live in, you can get something started called *initiative and referendum*. Here's a brief description of each way:

1. CONTACT SOMEONE WHO CAN HELP YOU. A law you want to pass is called a *bill* until it becomes a law. Even though you might write down your idea for the bill, it will still have to be rewritten in legal language. You can contact any of these people to help you put your bill in the proper form:

a. Contact a legislator. Legislators are the real lawmakers in your state government. Since you will eventually need a legislator to sponsor your bill, this is a good place to start.

The best legislator to contact is one who represents your district. Find out who your legislators are by calling your state house and asking. For a list of state houses and phone numbers, see pages 129–130.

Or you could contact a legislator who is on a committee that is studying your issue. To be polite, you should tell your district legislators if this is what you plan to do.

b. Contact your governor. He or she can begin the process of creating or changing a law. Be aware that governors are usually too busy to handle this. But if your governor happens to be a personal friend of yours, start here. Your governor can also tell you which people on his or her staff could help you.

c. Contact a staff person. Staff people are the workers and researchers at your state house. One of them could help you, too. But you must still find a legislator to sponsor your bill.

2. START THE INITIATIVE AND REFERENDUM PROCESS. Initiative and referendum is a way that some states share lawmaking power with the people.

Let's say that the people decide they want a new law, or a change in an existing law. Or they want to challenge a bill passed by the legislature before it becomes a law.

To do this, they collect a required number of signatures on a petition. This is called an *initiative*. (This *formal* petition process is different from the *informal* one described on pages 50–53.)

Next, the petition goes to the legislature for their consideration, or directly to the people for a vote. This vote is called a *referendum*.

What's your part in this process? Here are two ideas:

a. Find out if your state provides for this shared lawmaking power.

These are the states and jurisdictions that do:

Alaska	North Dakota
Arizona	Ohio
Arkansas	Oklahoma
California	Oregon
Colorado	South Dakota
Idaho	Utah
Maine	Washington
Massachusetts	Wyoming
Michigan	District of Columbia
Missouri	(Washington, D.C.)
Montana	Guam
Nebraska	North Mariana Islands
Nevada	

These are the states and jurisdictions where voters can challenge a bill that has already been passed by their legislature:

Alaska	New Mexico
Arizona	North Dakota
Arkansas	Ohio
California	Oklahoma
Colorado	Oregon
Idaho	South Dakota
Kentucky	Utah
Maine	Washington State
Maryland	Wyoming
Massachusetts	District of Columbia
Michigan	(Washington, D.C.)
Missouri	Guam
Montana	North Mariana Islands
Nebraska	Puerto Rico
Nevada	

Contact your governor's office to find out if your state has initiative and referendum. If it does, find out the rules for your state. (Each state has its own specific rules for initiative and referendum.) Or go to the library and study your *State Code*.

If your state doesn't have initiative and referendum, you might ask, "Why not?"

b. Carry your petition among the voters and gather signatures. Kids can't sign formal petitions. Only residents who are registered voters can. But unless your state has an age requirement for circulating a petition, there's nothing to stop you from carrying yours among voters. You would definitely need adult help with this, however.

What happens if your petition gets the required number of signatures? That depends on the state you live in. In some states, the proposed law or change goes directly to a vote without having to pass through the legislature first. In other states, it goes straight to the legislature, so they have time to change or oppose it before people vote on it.

In either case, for your petition to become a law, a majority of the people must vote for it.

HOW A BILL BECOMES A STATE LAW

1. THE BILL IS PREPARED

2. INTRODUCED IN ONE HOUSE IN THE LEGISLATURE (YOUR LEGISLATURE MAY HAVE ONLY ONE HOUSE)

3. REVIEWED BY THE RULES COMMITTEE

4. SENT FOR FIRST PRINTING

5. EXAMINED BY THE STANDING COMMITTEE

6. PRESENTED AT A PUBLIC HEARING (HERE'S WHERE YOU CAN HAVE INPUT)

7. DEBATED ON THE HOUSE FLOOR

8. SENT TO THE OTHER HOUSE IN THE LEGIS-LATURE (UNLESS YOUR LEGISLATURE HAS ONLY ONE HOUSE)

9. EXAMINED BY THE STANDING COMMITTEE

10. PRESENTED AT A PUBLIC HEARING (HERE'S WHERE YOU CAN HAVE INPUT)

11. DEBATED ON THE HOUSE FLOOR

12. SENT FOR FINAL PRINTING

13. SENT TO GOVERNOR FOR SIGNATURE

14. THE BILL IS NOW LAW

Jackson kids learn how to pass laws at the Utah State Capitol. At left is Representative Ted Lewis.

Courtesy Gary McKellar, *Deseret News*

Amending Your State Constitution

Have you read your state constitution lately? If you haven't, maybe you should. You just might think of a way to improve it.

A change to a constitution (state or federal) is called an *amendment*. If you've identified a problem, done your research, and decided that the best solution is an amendment to your state constitution, here's some information to get you started.

One important point: This is a difficult process, so you'll need lots of people on your team.

There are four basic ways a constitutional amendment can be proposed:

1. The state legislature may propose an amendment and submit it to the people for a vote.

2. In 17 states, the people may suggest an amendment by petition (initiative) and vote on it in a state election (referendum). The states are:

Arizona	Montana
Arkansas	Nebraska
California	Nevada
Colorado	North Dakota
Florida	Ohio
Illinois	Oklahoma
Massachusetts	Oregon
Michigan	South Dakota
Missouri	

If you live in one of these states, here is where you could play an important role. You would need to contact a government official (governor, legislator, or staff person), the same as you would if you wanted to initiate or change a state law.

3. In some states, constitutional conventions may adopt amendments, if the people vote to ratify them.

4. A constitutional commission may propose an amendment. It must then be approved by the legislature before it is put before the people for a vote.

LOBBYING:
THE ART OF PERSUASION

How can you convince lawmakers to vote for your bill? By *lobbying* them—the really fun part of the process.

A *lobbyist* is anyone who tries to convince a lawmaker to vote for or against a particular issue. In some states, a lobbyist is a professional who is paid for his work. He must officially register with the state. In other states, anyone can lobby by picking up the phone or showing up at the state house and chewing the fat with her local senator.

The word "lobbyist" comes from the practice of standing in the state house lobby while trying to get lawmakers' votes. Much lobbying still occurs outside the senate and house chambers.

As a lobbyist, you can have a lot of power, even if you're "just a kid." Because you won't always be a kid. Someday you'll be a voter. Lawmakers realize this, and most of them also feel the need to represent the views of all of their constituents, including you.

> **❝ A president only tells congress what they should do. Lobbyists tell 'em what they will do. ❞**
>
> *Will Rogers*

Should you try lobbying? Only if you have a real problem and a real solution to present. Lawmakers are under a lot of pressure to consider all the *legislation* (laws) and *appropriations* (ways state money will be spent) that come before them during each legislative session. Their time is too valuable for you to tie it up simply for a learning experience.

Let's assume that you *do* have a good idea. Here are some tips to get you started as a lobbyist.

Tips for Successful Lobbying

1. MAKE SURE YOU HAVE RESEARCHED YOUR ISSUE. Know what you're talking about—whether it's an issue you're introducing, or one that someone else has introduced and you want to support (or oppose).

2. START LOBBYING EARLY. The best time is well before your state's legislative session begins. Much legislation gets *tabled* (put aside) because time runs out before it can be considered.

If you begin early enough, present your issue to *interim committees*—committees which meet between sessions. This will give you a head start on getting attention for your problem.

Interim committees often meet on weekends or three or four days a month throughout the year. Much legislation is shaped in these committees. You can appear at these meetings to speak about your cause or to get help from members.

3. FIND A SPONSOR. Look for a legislator who will support your cause and help you through the process.

If possible, choose a legislator from your district, one who believes in your cause and wants to help. She will have experts on her staff to research your project at no cost to you. Her staff will rewrite your ideas in legal language and proper bill format. Your sponsor will also introduce your bill to legislators and speak in favor of it.

4. BUILD COALITIONS OF SUPPORT. Find others who are concerned about your issue (other schools? agencies? youth groups? parents?). Organize them. Let them know what you're planning to do. Ask them to help.

5. IDENTIFY YOUR OPPOSITION. Find out who might throw tacks in your path.

For example, if you're trying to put through a clean air bill, industries who pollute the air might not be in favor of correcting the problem, since it costs money to modify or replace polluting smokestacks. Don't ignore them. Meet with them and be willing to hear their side of the issue. Include their point of view in your bill.

Identifying your opposition also saves valuable time. Lawmakers will want to know how the other side feels before considering your idea.

6. ASK FOR MORE THAN YOU THINK YOU MIGHT GET. Then be willing to compromise.

7. ACQUAINT YOURSELF WITH THE RULES COMMITTEE. Each house has one, which acts as the "gatekeeper" for legislation. The rules committee decides which *standing committee* will investigate bills.

Standing committees (also called *permanent committees*) are the workhorses of the legislature. They cover areas like education, natural resources, health, social services, transportation, business and labor rules, and so on. You can usually go before these committees to speak for your cause.

As the legislative session draws near to the end, the rules committee can bypass standing committees to save bills from being tabled.

8. ACQUAINT YOURSELF WITH THE APPROPRIATIONS PROCESS. This is important if you want to have a say in how state money is spent.

The *appropriations committee* decides how the budget pie is sliced after the governor makes his or her recommendations. It is usually made up of lawmakers from both houses. Your state may have several appropriations committees to study needs in major areas—the courts, business, labor, energy, education, and so on. A senior appropriations committee prepares a final budget act for approval by lawmakers.

9. PREPARE ONE OR MORE POSTERS TO BRING TO COMMITTEE MEETINGS. (Check first to see if posters are allowed. Sometimes they aren't.) Your poster should present, reinforce, and clarify your idea in a visual way.

a. Make the printing large enough so the whole committee can read it from a distance.

b. Vary the print sizes. Your main heading should be in the largest printing.

c. Use color for more impact.

d. Try to stick to *one* main idea per poster. If you have several ideas to present, make several posters.

e. During the committee meetings, don't forget to use your poster. Point to it. Explain it. Repeat the idea presented on it.

10. PREPARE A ONE-PAGE FLYER TO HAND TO EACH LAWMAKER YOU LOBBY. Your flyer should include:

a. your bill number, title, and content (what the bill says)

b. your sponsor's name and title

c. your name, or the name of the group you are representing

d. a "needs statement"—your reasons for supporting (or opposing) the bill

e. your solution (which may be the bill itself)

f. your request for support (or, if you are opposing the bill, your request that the legislator join you in opposing it)

Make your flyer interesting to look at. Vary the print size, use color, add humor if appropriate. Legislators get a lot of flyers supporting or opposing bills. You want yours to stand out from the crowd.

If you think it's absolutely necessary, you could add *supporting material* (more pages). But legislators don't have much time to read large packets of information. One page is more likely to get their attention.

Page 105 is an example of a flyer the Jackson kids prepared in support of their Hazardous Waste Superfund. Page 106 shows part of the actual legislation after it was rewritten in legal language and passed.

11. SEND THANK-YOU NOTES TO THE PEOPLE WHO HELP YOU. This includes your sponsor, committee members, other legislators you lobby who agree to support your cause.

12. REMEMBER THAT GOOD PUBLIC RELATIONS ARE ESSENTIAL AT EVERY STEP OF THE WAY. Never speak discourteously, even if your contact is rude. Never argue or threaten. A polite attitude might pave the way for a future success, even from your opposition.

Above all, be yourself. Be a kid! You don't have to take legislators to dinner to win them over.

Jackson students testify in the Utah Legislature, House Standing Committee, in support of their Hazardous Waste Superfund. Representative Ted Lewis is at left.

Photos courtesy Dan Miller, *Salt Lake Tribune*

HB 199 State Contributory Superfund

for voluntary contributions

TO HELP CLEAN UP HAZARDOUS WASTE IN UTAH

Sponsored by: Ted Lewis   Co-sponsored by: Olene Walker

It will cost the state NOTHING.
It will benefit everyone

Initiated in behalf of Jackson Elementary students in the Extended Learning Program

UTAH SCENE

1. Utah has no superfund to clean up hazardous waste.
2. There are approximately 152 sites on the CERCLA list to be investigated as potentially hazardous places in Utah.
3. A 1987 report out of Washington D.C. ranked Utah 45th in the nation in developing environmental programs, including handling of hazardous waste.

DANGERS OF HAZARDOUS WASTE

1. It can cause birth defects, brain damage, neurological disorders, and many other kinds of diseases.
2. It can leak down and contaminate ground water, and then we drink it.
3. It can contaminate the air we breathe by being blown by the wind.
4. It can also contaminate the soils. Animals can eat food grown on contaminated soils. Then the chemicals can enter the food chain.

WHAT JACKSON KIDS HAVE DONE ALREADY

1. We held a Christmas Shop and White Elephant Sale and raised $486.22 which we would like to contribute to the fund.
2. At the beginning of January we mailed out about 550 letters to industries, environmental groups, businesses, and service organizations asking them if they would like to send pledges to contribute to this State Contributory fund IF IT IS PASSED. We have received over $2,192.00 in pledges thus far, for a total of $2,678.22.

PLEASE SUPPORT OUR BILL

HAZARDOUS WASTE FUND FOR VOLUNTARY CONTRIBUTIONS

1988

GENERAL SESSION

Enrolled Copy

By Ted D. Lewis

H.B. No. 199

Olene S. Walker

AN ACT RELATING TO SOLID AND HAZARDOUS WASTE; DIRECTING THE
DIVISION OF ENVIRONMENTAL HEALTH TO DEPOSIT ANY
VOLUNTARY CONTRIBUTIONS FOR THE CLEANUP OF HAZARDOUS
WASTE SITES AS DEDICATED CREDITS.
THIS ACT AFFECTS SECTIONS OF UTAH CODE ANNOTATED 1953 AS
FOLLOWS:

AMENDS:
26-14-20, AS ENACTED BY CHAPTER 176, LAWS OF UTAH 1985
Be it enacted by the Legislature of the state of Utah:
Section 1. Section 26-14-20, Utah Code Annotated 1953,
as enacted by Chapter 176, Laws of Utah 1985, is amended to
read:
26-14-20. (1) All money received by the state under
Section 26-14-19, and any voluntary contributions received
for the cleanup of hazardous waste sites, shall be
deposited by the Division of Environmental Health as
dedicated credits for the purposes outlined in Section 26-
14-19. Any unexpended balance at the end of the fiscal
year is nonlapsing.
(2) The director shall submit an annual report to the
Legislature which includes any investigation or abatement
action taken for which disbursements were made or
obligated, the amounts disbursed or obligated, and the
method and amount of any reimbursements.

LOBBYING IN PERSON

1. Get permission from your sponsor and set up a time to lobby.

Find out from your sponsor if there are any rules for lobbying. For example, do you have to register? Do you have to stay in certain areas?

2. Copy and fill out the lobbying in person form on page 169. This will help you to organize your thoughts and be prepared. Make copies of the form to take along. Bring copies of your flyer, too.

3. Prepare a three-minute (or shorter) speech to give each lawmaker you plan to lobby. (See pages 40–41 for tips.)

4. Dress and behave conservatively. Even though you might feel more comfortable in your favorite stretched-out tee shirt that says, "Nuke it all and start over," don't wear it to your state house.

5. Arrive on time, but don't expect the legislators to be on time. They may be voting on other measures, or they may be involved in a crisis. Wait patiently.

6. For each legislator you lobby, ask, "May I have your support?" This question requires an answer or commitment from the legislator. Make a note of his response on your lobbying in person form. If the answer is "no" or "maybe," stay calm. Don't act upset, disappointed, or angry. Above all, don't argue. Allow the legislator to express his opinion. You can lobby him again later, by phone or letter.

7. Tell the legislator if you are from his district. Your cause is stronger if you are a constituent.

8. Later, send thank-you notes to the people who help you—your sponsor, and anyone else who helps to set up your lobbying experience.

Jackson student Craig Dixon lobbies Utah Representative Irby Satterfield.

Courtesy Dan Miller, *Salt Lake Tribune*

IT TAKES 14 MUSCLES TO SMILE AND 72 TO FROWN.

Save energy. Smile!

❝ You cannot shake hands with a clenched fist. ❞

Indira Gandhi

LOBBYING BY TELEPHONE

1. Get a list of lawmakers' telephone numbers, both at home and at the state house. Your sponsor can probably get this list for you. During a legislative session, lawmakers try to make themselves easy to reach.

2. Copy and fill out the lobbying by phone form on page 170. This will help you to organize your thoughts and be prepared. Make copies of the form to use when you call.

3. The best time to call is just before the bill is placed on the agenda for voting. Your sponsor can let you know when this will be.

4. Call during the day, because many legislators might travel far away at night, requiring a long-distance phone call for you.

5. For each legislator you call, ask, "May I have your support?" Note her response on your form. If the answer is "no" or "maybe," plan to lobby that legislator again in person or by mail.

6. If the lawmaker isn't there when you call, leave a message and a phone number where she can return your call.

7. Keep a list of how each lawmaker plans to vote. This will give you a good idea of how strong your case is—and which legislators you should keep lobbying.

LOBBYING BY TESTIFYING

To *testify* means to go before a group or committee and speak in support of your cause. It's a great way to lobby because you can reach several people at a time.

Be aware that your issue will be openly debated. Legislators will discuss both sides.

Before the lawmakers are in session, you can speak before interim committee meetings. Don't forget this important step.

After your bill has been assigned to a standing committee, you could appear to testify at their public meeting, if one is scheduled. Tell your sponsor so that you can get whatever permission might be necessary.

Testifying before the chambers of the legislature when it is in session is not often permitted because of time limitations. Check with your sponsor. Jackson kids testified on the floor of the Utah Senate twice. Anything is possible!

Wherever you testify, here are some helpful tips to keep in mind:

1. Contact your sponsor and get permission to testify. Set up an appointed time. Find out if there are any rules you have to follow. For example, are posters allowed? How much time can you take?

2. Copy and fill out the lobbying by testifying form on page 171. This will help you to organize your thoughts and be prepared. (You can speak alone, or several of you can divide the speech into parts and each take a part.) Bring copies of your flyer, too.

3. Several short speeches (one to three minutes each) are better than one long, boring speech. The lobbying by testifying form can help you limit yourself.

You may add supporting material, but only if it's necessary. Lawmakers appreciate brief, concise statements.

Jackson kids testify on the floor of the Utah Senate to ask for passage of their Hazardous Waste Fund bill, HB199.

Courtesy Gary McKellar, *Deseret News*

4. Dress conservatively. Remember that your smile is the most impressive thing you can wear (and the most persuasive).

5. Always call your state house before leaving to testify. Schedules change suddenly. The discussion of your bill could be delayed.

6. Arrive on time. When you arrive, sign up to testify, unless your sponsor does it for you.

7. If a committee member asks you a question you don't fully understand, simply restate your purpose. Don't argue. Whatever you say will go on the record.

8. Be aware that your issue will be openly debated. Legislators will discuss both sides.

9. Ask for the committee's support before you sit down.

10. Later, send thank-you notes to your sponsor and the committee members.

IMPORTANT
• • • • • • • • •

If a committee member asks you if you would accept a change in the bill, say that you must talk with your group before you can answer that question.

MORE WAYS TO LOBBY

1. You can also *lobby by letter*. See page 29 for tips you can use and adapt for this purpose.

2. And you can *lobby the national government*— you don't have to stop at the state level. Think big! The process is basically the same as for lobbying your state government.

❝ You gain strength, courage, and confidence by every experience in which you really stop to look fear in the face... You must do the thing you think you cannot do. ❞

Eleanor Roosevelt

Ross Misher

Boca Raton, Florida. Ross Misher was only 13 years old when his father was murdered. But while this experience stole a hunk of his childhood, it also turned him into a leader.

"One of my father's employees went out on his lunch hour and purchased a handgun with the same ease as buying a cup of coffee," Ross explains. "He returned from lunch, and after work he killed my father and then killed himself. We do not know why. We never will. All I do know is for the rest of my life, a part of me will always be lying there, dead on the floor...

"I think about the 59 other families that went through the same exact thing I did...60 a day, every day...If a person cannot wait a short period of time to receive a gun, I do not think he needs it for the right reasons."

Ross testified before a U.S. Senate Subcommittee in support of requiring a "cooling-off period" for anyone purchasing a handgun. That would give someone seven days to re-think a violent act before getting a chance to commit it with a gun. Ross also wrote a piece of handgun control legislation in Boys State which was submitted to the Florida State Legislature. He debated his views on national television and founded the Palm Beach County Handgun Control Network.

While Ross was becoming a leader, he was also being a kid. He was an honor student and president of his junior class. He ran all the pep rallies for his school, and even wrote the high school song.

When Ross moved on to George Washington University, he carried his campaign with him, starting "Students Against Hand Gun Violence." It's the first group of its type to hit a college campus.

Although Ross sounds like a superhero, he's the kind of guy you'd love to meet. He's very humble and unpretentious. He acts as though he's just doing his job.

Why does he do it? "I don't think I'll ever end this ongoing fight," he says. "It's become a part of my life. I owe it not only to my community; I owe it to my dad."

He has some advice—and an invitation—for you: "Join me, youth of America. Go out there and do it. Anything you see a need for, don't let others do it. Do it yourself.

"If you can touch one person in any way, you can save the world." ◉

Ross Misher tells an audience about his gun-control cause.

RESOLUTIONS

> **Resolve to create a good future. It's where you'll spend the rest of your life.**
>
> *Charles Franklin Kettering*

Resolutions aren't just those wonderful plans for self-improvement you make on New Year's Day and forget the day after. Resolutions can be used to change policies in your city, state, and nation.

There are two main types of resolutions:

1. A FORMAL STATEMENT urging a plan of action. For example, a legislature may decide to ask a committee to investigate seat belt safety.

Kids can also initiate a resolution in either the house or the senate.

2. A COMMENDATION of appreciation. For example, a mayor might make a resolution recognizing the contributions of an individual or group.

Resolutions can begin in the house, the senate, or the state house. Or the house and the senate may write a *joint resolution* together. Add the governor to the house and the senate, and you've got a *concurrent resolution.*

Resolutions have no *binding effect.* In other words, they are not laws. However, Jackson kids began the initiative process with a resolution proposing a Utah State Superfund. Their resolution was made into House Bill 199. The kids lobbied legislators to vote for their bill, and it became a law. Later, the city council and mayor gave the kids a commendation for their work.

If they can do it, so can you.

Tips for Successful Resolutions

1. Start by contacting your state senator or representative. He'll work with you if he's interested in your idea. You could also initiate your resolution with a staff person or with your governor, but your best bet is your legislator.

2. Your resolution *must not conflict with existing laws and rules.* Your legislator can help you find out if yours is in the clear.

3. Because resolutions may cost several hundreds of dollars of taxpayer money to process, some legislators grow impatient with the time they require. Don't let this stop you from using this process. Just be sure that your cause is worthwhile.

4. If you're involved in a city-wide or state-wide campaign over a problem which affects many people, get local governments involved. By doing this, you will build a strong coalition of support.

Many cities and towns present resolutions in their local meetings. If they are approved there, they will probably be introduced in the next law-making session. Include every group or agency you think might be interested in your resolution.

5. Be aware that resolutions are open to debate—people might argue against them. Your resolution might be amended or changed by legislators. Don't take any of this personally.

How to Write a Resolution

Resolutions follow a very specific form. Yours will get better attention if you show that you know the form.

First, the basics:
▶ Your resolution must be in writing.
▶ Keep it concise.
▶ Double-space or triple-space to allow for notes or changes.
▶ Number the lines for easy reference.

A resolution has two parts: the *preamble* and the *conclusion*. The preamble states the need and reasons for your resolution. The conclusion is based on the reasons given in the preamble.

1. WRITING THE PREAMBLE.
a. State the need and reasons for your resolution.
b. Start each clause (reason) with "Whereas, The..."
c. You may write more than one clause.
d. End each clause with a comma or a semicolon followed by the word "and." The last clause should end with "therefore" or "therefore, be it..."

2. WRITING THE CONCLUSION.
a. Write your conclusion in statement form. Start with "<u>Resolved</u>, That..."
b. You may write more than one concluding statement.
c. Each statement that follows the first should begin, "<u>Be it further resolved</u>..." Or the first concluding statement should end, "and be it further," with "<u>Resolved</u>" starting each new statement.
d. The last statement should read, "and be it finally <u>Resolved</u>, That..."
e. The word <u>Resolved</u> must be underlined and followed with a comma. The word "That" must begin with a capital T.

All underlining, punctuation, and sentence structure must remain consistent throughout the resolution.

When your legislator presents your resolution, he will take the floor and state, "I move the adoption of the following resolution," or "I offer the following resolution." Then he will read your resolution and hand it to the chairperson.

You can copy and use the resolution form on page 172 to write your own resolution. Find examples of real resolutions on the next two pages.

Here's an example:

1 Whereas, The...(text of the first preamble clause), and

2 Whereas, The...(text of the second preamble clause), and

3 Whereas, The...(text of the last preamble clause), therefore, be it

4 <u>Resolved</u>, That...(stating the action to be taken), and be it further

5 <u>Resolved</u>, That...(stating further action to be taken), and be it finally

6 <u>Resolved</u>, That...(stating still further action to be taken).

I OFFER THE FOLLOWING RESOLUTION...

Whereas hazardous waste is defined as wastes that are harmful to living things or the environment...

Resolution

We the students at Jackson Elementary would like to initiate the following resolution:

1 Whereas, Hazardous waste is defined as wastes that are harmful to living things or environment when improperly handled; and

2 Whereas, The State of Utah has no state superfund to clean up hazardous waste; and

3 Whereas, The State of Utah has approximately 152 sites on the CERCLA list of sites to be investigated; and

4 Whereas, The State of Utah has ten sites on the National Priorities List awaiting cleanup; and

5 Whereas, In the State of Utah in 1986, 3,000,000 tons of hazardous waste was handled by treatment, storage, and disposal; therefore be it

6 <u>Resolved</u>, That the State of Utah create a State Contributory Superfund designated for cleanup of hazardous waste to which a party can voluntarily donate money.

SALT LAKE CITY CORPORATION

Resolution

A JOINT RESOLUTION OF THE
CITY COUNCIL AND MAYOR OF
SALT LAKE CITY, UTAH

Resolution No. _____ of 1988

WHEREAS,   the Extended Learning Program students of Jackson Elementary have been very active in community affairs; and

WHEREAS,   they have worked with local, state and national agencies to clean up a toxic waste sight; and

WHEREAS,   they drafted a bill to create a Superfund for the State of Utah to receive donations to help clean up the environment; and

WHEREAS,   they raised money to make the first contribution to the State Superfund; and

WHEREAS,   they have recently been honored by the Environmental Protection Agency in Washington, D. C.; and

WHEREAS,   they are continuing their efforts to enhance our community with a tree planting project.

NOW, THEREFORE BE IT RESOLVED by the City Council and Major Palmer DePaulis of Salt Lake City, Utah, that they do hereby congratulate the past and present students of the Jackson Elementary School Early Learning Program, and encourage the students to continue their community activity.

DATED this _____ day of December, 1988.

Mayor Palmer DePaulis

Tom Godfrey, Chairperson

Florence B. Bittner

L. Wayne Horrocks

Sydney Fonnesbeck

Alan G. Hardman

Roselyn N. Kirk

W. M. "Willie" Stoler

NATIONAL LAWS

You know that kids can make a difference at the local level. Even at the state level. But at the *national* level? Isn't that totally out of reach?

Jackson kids lobbied the national government to get kids included in the America the Beautiful Act of 1990. Because of their efforts, youth groups across the United States can now apply for matching grants of money to plant trees.

Maybe you have an idea for a new national law. Or maybe you know an old one that needs changing. Why not give it a try? You've got nothing to lose and much to gain from the experience.

Remember that constituents—people like you, your parents and neighbors, your teachers and friends—are a great source of ideas for initiating new laws or changing old laws.

> **Progress involves risk. You can't steal second base and keep your foot on first.**
>
> *Frederick Wilcox*

Learn about the U.S. Government

The United States government has three branches:

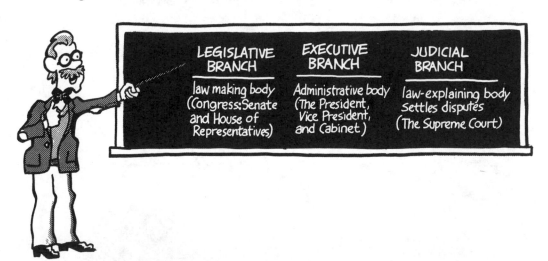

LEGISLATIVE BRANCH	EXECUTIVE BRANCH	JUDICIAL BRANCH
law making body (Congress: Senate and House of Representatives)	Administrative body (The President, Vice President, and Cabinet)	law-explaining body settles disputes (The Supreme Court)

Have you been learning about the U.S. government in school? If not, now's the time. Especially if you're thinking about initiating or changing a national law. You need to know what you're talking about!

Look for these books at your library reference desk:

▶ *The Congressional Directory* (U.S. Government Printing Office, published annually). Listings and information about members of Congress and their staffs.

▶ *The Congressional Record* (U.S. Government Printing Office, published daily). Tells what happens in Congress each day (bills introduced, bills voted on, hearings scheduled, etc.)

▶ *Encyclopedia of Governmental Advisory Organizations* (Gale Research, 1993). A guide to over 5,400 committees, including Presidential, congressional, and public advisory committees, government-related boards, panels, commissions, task forces, conferences, more. Find the most recent volume.

▶ *The Federal Register* (U.S. Government Printing Office, published daily). Information about executive and agency meetings, rule making, hearings, comment periods, etc.

▶ *The United States Government Manual* (U.S. Government Printing Office, published annually). Tells how the federal government is organized, describes duties of different offices, etc.

You may want copies of these for yourself:

▶ *How Our Laws Are Made* (U.S. Government Printing Office, 1986). Write or call: U.S. Government Printing Office, Washington, D.C. 20402; (202) 783-3238. Ask for Document No. 99-158.

▶ *Making An Issue Of It: The Campaign Handbook* (League of Women Voters, 1976). A citizen action guide; small fee.

BOOKS FOR YOUNG READERS

☞ *Congress* by Harold Coy, revised by Barbara L. Dammann (Franklin Watts, 1981). About Congress and committees, the President, courts, lobbies and pressure groups, media impact, and the story of a bill. Easy to read.

☞ *I Want To Know About the United States Senate* by Senator Charles Percy (Doubleday, 1976). The duties and life of a senator.

How to Initiate or Change a National Law

Suppose you have chosen a problem and researched it. Your solution is to go for a new national law, or a change in an existing law. (Take another look at "Ten Tips for Taking Social Action" on pages 12–13.) Here's how to do it.

1. CONTACT SOMEONE WHO CAN HELP YOU. If you wanted to initiate or change a state law, you'd contact someone in state government. If your goal is a national law, you'll need someone in national government on your side.

ASK FOR ADVICE (AND WRITE IT DOWN)

As you're looking for people to help you, take time to ask for their opinions and advice on your project. Do they think your idea is a good one? Why or why not? Do you need to change anything to make it work? Get names, phone numbers, and addresses of other people who might help you.

---

a. Contact a member of Congress. These are the real lawmakers in national government. And you will eventually need a member of Congress to sponsor your bill.

The best person to pick is one who represents your state. Every state has two senators, and you could pick one of these. Or you could choose a state representative instead. How many representatives your state has depends on your state's population. For example, if you live in Maine, you have two representatives; if you live in California, you have as many as 45.

You could also choose a member of Congress who is on a committee that is studying your issue (housing, transportation, etc.). Even though this person might not represent your state, she still might be willing to help you. To be polite, you should tell your state senators and representatives if this is what you plan to do.

b. Contact the President, Vice President, or a cabinet member. They can't make any laws, but they can suggest changes. And they can offer advice and support. If you can convince any of them to join your team, they will be powerful players.

c. Contact a staff person or department member. As in state government, these are the workers and researchers. They might be easier for you to reach, and they can help you begin the process of initiating or changing a law.

PICK UP THE PHONE!

☞ Federal government switchboard operators will connect you with specific departments. Call (202) 224-3121.

☞ If you'd like to speak to members of Congress, committees, or subcommittees, call the U.S. Capitol at (202) 224-3121.

☞ To find out the status of legislation and dates of hearings, call (202) 225-1772, then ask for the department you want to speak to.

☞ And if you feel like leaving a message for the President, call the White House at (202) 456-1414.

Addresses and phone numbers for other government offices are found on pages 131–135.

---

2. BUILD SUPPORT FOR YOUR BILL. Find other people to join your team: other kids, schools, state officials, agencies, media people. You could conduct surveys to find out how other people think, and pass petitions to gather names of people who agree with you. Try to get media coverage for your cause. (See pages 66–77 for tips, ideas, and examples.) Convincing TV and newspaper reporters to tell your story will usually encourage all sorts of people to support your efforts.

3. WORK WITH YOUR OPPOSITION. You should never neglect this step! There will always be people who disagree with you. Ignoring them might keep you from reaching your goal. It might also keep you from discovering what you have in common, and maybe even joining forces to work together.

At the very least, you might be able to convince these people not to interfere with what you're trying to do. And you'll learn to see their side of the issue, too.

4. LOBBY FOR YOUR LEGISLATION. Try to convince lawmakers to support your bill or proposed change. You can lobby by phone, letter, or FAX, if you have access to a facsimile machine.

Lobbying in person might seem difficult without a private plane. Then again, Audrey Chase flew to Washington, D.C., with her mom and lobbied in person for the "Leaf It To Us" tree amendment. (You read Audrey's story on page 11.)

Other Jackson kids have flown many different places. How do they finance their travels? Usually they find sponsors to pay their expenses—supporters in business or industry. Or they fundraise in other ways.

❝ Congress shall make no law... abridging the freedom of speech, or of the press; or the right of the people peaceably to assemble, and to petition the government for a redress of grievances. ❞

First Amendment,
Constitution of the United States, 1791.

"LEAF it to US!"

Jackson Elementary
750 W. 200 N.
Salt Lake City, Ut.
84116

The President
The White House
Washington D.C. 20500

Dear President Bush:

Hi! We would like money for kids to plant trees on public grounds across the nation. We heard you want to put up $60,000,000 for planting trees. That's exactly what we would like to do. Could some of it be used for a Children's Fund for kids across the nation?

Kids could match 10 to 20% of the money they took out. The kids could apply for grants. The money could be kept in Washington D.C.

We would not like to use an Adult fund, we would like it to be just for kids.

<u>One tree</u> in it's average 50 yr. lifetime contributes $162,000 worth of air pollution control. They also recycle water, and prevent soil erosion.

We've already talked to the honorable Senator Orrin Hatch and asked him to pass some legislation or set aside some money for kids. We're already planting trees in Utah. We have already gone to our own legislature.

Is there anything more we can do?

Trees are a Tree-mendous

Con-Tree-bution!

Sincerely,

Shane Price   Audrey Chase
Jeremy Maestas   Micki J Nay   Darren P.
Sharee Bright   Richelle Warner
Shannon Ackman Richard Tehero

THE WHITE HOUSE
WASHINGTON

April 25, 1990

Dear Girls and Boys:

Senator Orrin Hatch was kind enough to write me about your wonderful "Leaf-It-To-Us — Children's Crusade for Trees Project." As I read the material from you, your principal, and the Senator, I was impressed by your creativity and initiative. Your enthusiasm and hard work are an example for all Americans to follow.

As you watch your trees grow, you will be able to take great pride in the contribution you have made to improving our environment. Your forestry project represents a lasting investment in the future.

Mrs. Bush joins me in commending you for your efforts. You can be certain that we will tell others of the time, effort, and energy you have put into this worthy project. Keep up the good work, and God bless you.

Sincerely,

George Bush

Pupils of Jackson Elementary School
Extended Learning Program
750 West 200 North
Salt Lake City, Utah 84116

Amending the U.S. Constitution

Suppose the solution to your problem is to try for an amendment to the United States Constitution. This is *very* difficult to accomplish—but that doesn't mean it's impossible.

Are you interested? Some kids are.

There are two basic ways an amendment can be proposed to the Constitution of the United States:

1. Congress can propose an amendment with
   ▶ a 2/3 vote of both houses, and
   ▶ approval of 3/4 of the state legislatures, or
   ▶ conventions in 3/4 of the states.

2. Legislatures of 2/3 of the states can call a convention for proposing amendments. For an amendment to be accepted, it must be approved by
   ▶ 3/4 of the state legislatures, or
   ▶ conventions in 3/4 of the states.

As a kid, you could begin the process by contacting a member of Congress from your state. But you should probably collect thousands of signatures on a petition to show support for your amendment. You could also start by contacting the President, the Vice President, or a staff person, just as you would to initiate or change a law.

Some fifth graders in New Jersey are trying to amend the Constitution. Here is their amazing story.

Kids Against Pollution (KAP)

Closter, New Jersey. While studying the Bill of Rights, a group of energetic fifth graders in teacher Nick Byrne's class lifted their noses from their books to ask, "How can we use our right to free expression?"

"Choose a topic and write to newspapers, magazines, and public officials," Byrne answered.

Since pollution seemed to cloud the pages of everything they read, Byrne's students chose that as their project. But they weren't satisfied with just writing letters. These kids at Tenakill School in Closter, New Jersey, went a bit further than that.

In 1987, they founded a networking information organization called "KAP"—Kids Against Pollution. They created their own logo and motto: "Save the Earth—not just for us but for future generations."

As Cathy Bell, one of the original fifth-grade founders, explained, "I think pollution is more deadly than the threat of nuclear war. Because everyone knows about the prospect of that war, but pollution just sneaks up on you....Adults are running up a bill on their credit cards that my generation has to pay."

Three years later, KAP has grown to 600 groups in the United States, and it's still growing. KAP also has contacts in several countries around the world.

Rich Luzzi, a KAP kid, wrote a letter to students in the U.S.S.R. In return, he received an invitation to write for that country's *Campfire Magazine*. And kids from other countries are interested in starting KAP chapters.

Once or twice a year, KAP kids conduct a massive mailing to inform other students, teachers, and officials of their powerful environmental message. Recently, the group won grants to finance their information campaign, including $85,000 worth of IBM computer equipment from a program sponsored by IBM and *U.S. News & World Report.* Now the kids can really pound the keyboards to put out their newsletter and information packages.

But that's not all. KAP kids are also advocating the passage of a Constitutional Amendment (state *and* national) that would guarantee everyone the right to clean air, water, and land, and would encourage environmental education in schools. Having already spoken before local, state, and national government officials, they have carried their plea for a clean environment to many people.

If you're interested, you can help them by signing their nationwide petition. Find it on page 125. Make a photocopy, sign it, and send it to KAP. "If we get enough people," Cathy Bell says, "politicians are going to start to listen.

From a New Jersey classroom to a Constitutional amendment may seem impossibly far to go. But the KAP kids did it. They called it "free expression." How are *you* going to express yourself?

If you'd like to know more about KAP, write to: KAP, P.O. Box 775, Closter, New Jersey 07624. Send $10.00 to become a member. ☉

Tenakill School teacher Nick Byrne and his KAP students state their case for environmental education in the New York Assembly Standing Committee on Environmental Conservation in Albany, New York.

Courtesy *U.S. News & World Report*

Tenakill School
275 High Street
Closter, N.J.
07624

Founders
Lauren Abate
Edwin Baez
Catherine Bell
Deborah Biondo
Jeffrey Gross
Suzanne Hammerle
Christy Huppach
Tracy Katz
Jaime Kolacia
Peter Laudenback
Sharyn Miskovitz
Demetrios Philliou
Jason Pitofsky
Crystal Ranges
Eric Silverstein
Beth Ann
Terrafranca
Chuck Theurer
Kevin Wilson
Saskia Dystant
Mr. Nick Byrne
5th Grade Teacher

Honorary Founder
Mr. Walter Pevny

Honorary Members
Mrs. Claire
Crowley
Mrs. Connie Luzzi

Environmental Bill of Rights

Our legislators are mandated in the Preamble of our Constitution to provide for our general welfare. Because of this, we believe we are entitled, by law, to clean air, land and water.

It does not appear that our right to a clean environment is being upheld. Therefore, we propose that an amendment be made to our State and National Constitutions which will mandate specific environmental rules. In this way, because all legislators have taken an oath to uphold the constitution, they will be compelled to enact and enforce the law.

AIR

We have a right to clean air uncontaminated with the poisonous byproducts of industry. We have the right to an atmosphere free of chlorinated fluourocarbons and high levels of carbon monoxide both of which are, today, contributing to a global warming (also known as the "greenhouse effect"). Every reasonable means should be taken to promptly accomplish this task.

WATER

Water is the lifeblood of our planet. We have the right to uncontaminated drinking water, not water that is increasingly laden with toxins and industrial byproducts. We have the right to swim in our Nation's waterways, to see its shores free of waste from ocean dumping, to catch fish that are not laden with mercury, PCB's, lead, dioxin, or other substances harmful to life.

LAND

Our land is a precious resource. We cannot continue to dump our waste on it without taking the strictest precautions. There must be tighter control of dumping and the lining to landfills where landfills are necessary to prevent contamination of the water supply. Recycling must be made mandatory and recycled products should be encouraged through tax breaks and government purchasing. We must reduce the volume of waste by returning it to its manufacturers.

EDUCATION

Finally, Environmental Education should be a subject taught as a separate course for at least one month each year starting at kindergarten and culminating in the 12th grade. This course should be a practical one which emphasizes how we can conserve our resources and how to eliminate all forms of pollution.

ENVIRONMENTAL BILL OF RIGHTS PETITION

We the undersigned fully support Kids Against Pollution (KAP) in their effort to have their Environmental Bill of Rights adopted by both the state and national constitutions. Together we can achieve great goals. The areas addressed — AIR — WATER — LAND — EDUCATION — are important —"not just for us, but for future generations."

_____   _____

_____   _____

_____   _____

_____   _____

_____   _____

_____   _____

_____   _____

_____   _____

_____   _____

_____   _____

_____   _____

_____   _____

1. Photocopy. 2. Sign and have your friends sign. 3. Send to: KAP, P.O. Box 775, Closter, NJ 07624.

125

RESOURCES

STATE HOUSE CONTACTS:
CAPITALS, ZIP CODES, AND CENTRAL SWITCHBOARDS

State or Jurisdiction	Capital	Zip Code	Central Switchboard
Alabama	Montgomery	36130	205/261-2500
Alaska	Juneau	99811	907/465-2111
Arizona	Phoenix	85007	602/542-4900
Arkansas	Little Rock	72201	501/682-1010
California	Sacramento	95814	916/322-9900
Colorado	Denver	80203	303/866-5000
Connecticut	Hartford	06106	203/566-2211
Delaware	Dover	19901	302/739-4000
Florida	Tallahassee	32399	904/488-1234
Georgia	Atlanta	30334	404/656-2000
Hawaii	Honolulu	96813	808/548-2211
Idaho	Boise	83720	208/334-2411
Illinois	Springfield	62706	217/782-2000
Indiana	Indianapolis	46204	317/232-3140
Iowa	Des Moines	50319	515/281-5011
Kansas	Topeka	66612	913/296-0111
Kentucky	Frankfort	40601	502/564-3130
Lousiana	Baton Rouge	70804	504/342-6600
Maine	Augusta	04333	207/289-1110
Maryland	Annapolis	21401	301/858-3000
Massachusetts	Boston	02133	617/727-2121
Michigan	Lansing	48909	517/373-1837
Minnesota	St. Paul	55515	612/296-6013
Mississippi	Jackson	39215	601/359-1000
Missouri	Jefferson City	65101	314/751-2000
Montana	Helena	59620	406/444-2511
Nebraska	Lincoln	68509	402/471-2311
Nevada	Carson City	89710	702/687-6800
New Hampshire	Concord	03301	603/271-1110
New Jersey	Trenton	08625	609/292-4840
New Mexico	Santa Fe	87503	505/986-4300
New York	Albany	12224	518/474-2121
North Carolina	Raleigh	27611	919/733-1110
North Dakota	Bismarck	58505	701/224-2000
Ohio	Columbus	43215	614/466-2000

State or Jurisdiction	Capital	Zip Code	Central Switchboard
Oklahoma	Oklahoma City	73105	405/521-2011
Oregon	Salem	97310	503/378-8551
Pennsylvania	Harrisburg	17120	717/787-2121
Rhode Island	Providence	02903	401/277-2000
South Carolina	Columbia	29211	803/734-1000
South Dakota	Pierre	57501	605/773-3011
Tennessee	Nashville	37243	615/741-3011
Texas	Austin	78711	512/463-4630
Utah	Salt Lake City	84114	801/538-3000
Vermont	Montpelier	05609	802/828-1110
Virginia	Richmond	23219	804/786-0000
Washington	Olympia	98504	206/753-5000
West Virginia	Charleston	25305	304/348-3456
Wisconsin	Madison	53702	608/266-2211
Wyoming	Cheyenne	82002	307/777-7220
District of Columbia	Washington, D.C.	20004	202/727-1000
American Samoa	Pago Pago	96799	684/633-5231
Federated States of Micronesia	Kolonia	96941	NCS
Guam	Agana	96910	671/472-8931
Marshall Islands	Majuro	96960	NCS
No. Mariana Islands	Saipan	96950	NCS
Puerto Rico	San Juan	00904	809/721-6040
Republic of Belau	Koror	96940	NCS
Virgin Islands	Charlotte Amalie	00801	809/774-0880

NCS - No central switchboard

Adapted from *The Book of the States* (Kentucky: The Council of State Governments), 1992–93, with updated corrections, 1993. Used with permission.

U.S. GOVERNMENT OFFICES

The Yellow Book—Federal numbers, (202) 347-7757.

Capitol Hill operator, (202) 224-3121. Connects you to the Senate or House of Representatives offices. For all other government offices, call directory assistance, (202)555-1212.

THE GOVERNMENT OF THE UNITED STATES

THE CONSTITUTION

EXECUTIVE BRANCH

THE PRESIDENT
Executive Office of the President

White House Office
Office of Management and Budget
Council of Economic Advisors
National Security Council
Office of Policy Development
Office of National Drug Control Policy

National Critical Materials Council
Office of the U.S. Trade Representative
Council on Environmental Quality
Office of Science and Technology Policy
Office of Administration
National Space Council

THE VICE-PRESIDENT

LEGISLATIVE BRANCH

THE CONGRESS

Senate   **House**

Architect of the Capitol
United States Botanical Garden
General Accounting Office
Government Printing Office
Office of Technology Assessment
Congressional Budget Office
Copyright Royalty Tribunal
United States Tax Court

JUDICIAL BRANCH

THE SUPREME COURT OF THE UNITED STATES

United States Court of Appeals
United States District Courts
United States Claims Court
United States Court of Appeals
for the Federal Circuit
United States Court of Military Appeals
United States Court of Veteran Appeals
Administrative Office of the United States Courts
Federal Judicial Court

DEPARTMENT OF AGRICULTURE	DEPARTMENT OF COMMERCE	DEPARTMENT OF DEFENSE	DEPARTMENT OF EDUCATION
DEPARTMENT OF ENERGY	DEPARTMENT OF THE INTERIOR	DEPARTMENT OF JUSTICE	DEPARTMENT OF LABOR
DEPARTMENT OF STATE	DEPARTMENT OF TRANSPORTATION	DEPARTMENT OF THE TREASURY	DEPARTMENT OF VETERANS AFFAIRS
	DEPARTMENT OF HEALTH AND HUMAN SERVICES	DEPARTMENT OF HOUSING AND URBAN DEVELOPMENT	

SOURCE: *United States Government Manual*, 1989/90, Office of the Federal Register, U.S. Government Printing Office, Washington, D.C., p. 21.

Executive Branch

The President of the United States
White House Office
1600 Pennsylvania Ave.
Washington, D.C. 20500
(202) 456-1414
Chief administrator of the United States.

Vice President of the United States
Old Executive Office Bldg.
Washington, D.C. 20501
(202) 456-2326
President of the U.S. Senate;
    second in line to the Presidency.

Office of Management and Budget
Executive Office Bldg.
Washington, D.C. 20503
(202) 395-3080
Assists and advises the President in
    managing the executive branch;
    administers the federal budget.

Council of Economic Advisers
Old Executive Office Bldg.
Washington, D.C. 20500
(202) 395-5084
Analyzes the national economy; advises the
    President on economic policies.

National Security Council
Old Executive Office Bldg.
Washington, D.C. 20506
(202) 395-4974
Advises the President on issues involving
    military and national security.

Office of the United States Trade Representative
600 Seventeenth Street, N.W.
Washington, D.C. 20506
(202) 395-3230
Responsible for U.S. trade negotiations and trade
    policy; advises the President on trade policy.

Council on Environmental Quality
722 Jackson Place, N.W.
Washington, D.C. 20503
(202) 395-5750
Advises the President on environmental issues.

Office of National Drug Control Policy
750 17th Street, N.W.
Washington, D.C. 20500
(202) 467-9880
Information on policies to control illegal drugs.

Office of Science and Technology Policy
New Executive Office Bldg.
Washington D.C. 20500
(202) 456-7116
Advises the President on science and
    technology issues.

DEPARTMENTS

Department of Agriculture
Fourteenth Street and Independence Ave., S.W.
Washington D.C. 20250
(202) 720-8722
Works to market farm products; combats poverty, hunger, and malnutrition; works to improve the environment by protecting the soil, water, forests, etc.

Department of Commerce
Fourteenth Street
Between Constitution Ave. and E Street., N.W.
Washington, D.C. 20230
(202) 482-2000
Promotes international trade, economic growth, business growth, etc.

Department of Defense
The Pentagon
Washington, D.C. 20301-1155
(703) 545-6700
Provides the country's military forces.

Department of Education
400 Maryland Ave., S.W.
Washington, D.C. 20202
(202) 708-5366
Handles federal assistance to schools and educational programs.

Department of Energy
1000 Independence Ave., S.W.
Washington, D.C. 20585
(202) 586-5000
Deals with national energy use, including conservation and the nuclear weapons program.

Department of Health and Human Services
200 Independence Ave., S.W.
Washington, D.C. 20201
(202) 619-0257
The department most concerned with meeting human needs; deals with health issues, Social Security, etc.

Department of Housing and Urban Development
451 Seventh Street, S.W.
Washington, D.C. 20410
(202) 708-1422
Responsible for meeting the nation's housing needs, including insurance, rentals, low-income family dwellings, etc.

Department of the Interior
1849 C Street, N.W.
Washington, D.C. 20240
(202) 208-3100
Responsible for most of the nationally owned lands and resources, including parks, forests, wildlife, etc.

Department of Justice
Constitution Ave. and Tenth Street, N.W.
Washington, D.C. 20530
(202) 514-2000
The largest law firm in the United States; serves as counsel for all citizens. Works to uphold the law, safeguard consumers, etc.

Department of Labor
200 Constitution Ave., N.W.
Washington, D.C. 20210
(202) 219-5000
Works to improve the nation's employment rates and working conditions.

Department of State
2201 C Street, N.W.
Washington, D.C. 20520
(202) 647-4000
Advises the President on foreign policy matters.

Department of Transportation
400 Seventh Street, S.W.
Washington, D.C. 20590
(202) 366-4000
Makes national policy for highways, mass transit, railroads, airlines, waterways, oil and gas pipelines, etc.

Department of the Treasury
1500 Pennsylvania Ave., N.W.
Washington, D.C. 20220
(202) 622-2000
Sets money policies, including taxes; mints coins and currency.

Department of Veteran Affairs
810 Vermont Ave., N.W.
Washington, D.C. 20420
(202) 233-4000
Operates programs for veterans and their families (education, housing, medical care, etc.).

Legislative Branch

U.S. Senate and House of Representatives.
Write directly to individual senators and
representatives at these addresses:

The Senate
The Capitol
Washington, D.C. 20510

The House of Representatives
The Capitol
Washington, D.C. 20515

Reach any member of Congress and all committees and subcommittees by calling (202) 224-3121.

Legislative Status Office. For information on legislation in the House and the Senate, and dates of
committee hearings, call (202) 225-1772.

OTHER ORGANIZATIONS

Congressional Budget Office
Second and D Streets, S.W.
Washington, D.C. 20515
(202) 226-2621
Reports to Congress on the impact of the federal
budget.

Copyright Royalty Tribunal
1825 Connecticut Ave., N.W.
Suite 918
Washington, D.C. 20009
(202) 606-4400
Determines copyright royalty rates for records,
jukeboxes, some cable TV.

General Accounting Office
441 G Street, N.W.
Washington, D.C. 20548
(202) 512-3000
The investigative arm of Congress; concerned with
the use of public money.

Government Printing Office
North Capitol and H Streets, N.W.
Washington, D.C. 20410
(202) 512-0000
Printers of all government documents and
publications.

Library of Congress
101 Independence Ave., S.E.
Washington, D.C. 20540
(202) 707-5000
The national library—HUGE, and housed in many
buildings.

Office of Technology Assessment
Public Affairs and Congressional Affairs
600 Pennsylvania Ave., S.E.
Washington, D.C. 20510-8025
(202) 224-9241
Reports to Congress on science and technology as
they relate to government policies.

THE U.S. GOVERNMENT PRINTING OFFICE

The "GPO" publishes over 30,000 booklets, pam-
phlets, books, and other documents. If there is
a particular subject you're interested in, write to
the GPO at the address given above. They will
send you a list of their publications.

To order documents, write to: Superintendent
of Documents, U.S. Government Printing Office,
Washington, D.C. 20402. Or call (202) 783-3238.
*Be sure to include the document number when
ordering.*

You can phone in orders with a charge card by
calling (202) 783-3238.

Judicial Branch

Supreme Court of the United States

U.S. Supreme Court Bldg.
1 First Street, N.E.
Washington, D.C. 20543
(202) 479-3000, (202) 479-3011
The federal court which settles disputes of national importance; also hears appealed cases from lower courts.

U.S. Court of Appeals for the Federal Circuit

717 Madison Place, N.W.
Washington, D.C. 20439
(202) 633-6550
Handles cases which have been disputed in lower courts.

U.S. District Courts

333 Constitution Ave., N.W.
Washington, D.C. 20001
(202) 273-0555
Trial courts with general federal jurisdiction. Each state has at least one district court.

Federal Judicial Center

1 Columbus Circle, N.E.
Washington, D.C. 20002-8003
(202) 273-4000
Researches operation of U.S. courts for the public.

For a wealth of information on the United States government—its offices, departments, agencies, and services—see the latest edition of *Information U.S.A.* by Matthew Lesko (Penguin Books).

CONTACT GROUPS
FOR INFORMATION, NETWORKING, AND PROGRAMS

This section includes listings of many national groups. Contact them for more information, and for addresses of local chapters or groups.

This is not intended to be a comprehensive directory. Check your library reference desk for additional references. Also see:

▶ *Directory of American Youth Organizations: A Guide To Over 400 Clubs, Groups, Troops, Teams, Societies, Lodges, and More For Young People* by Judith B. Erickson (Free Spirit Publishing, updated every two years). Lists service groups, organizations for peace and global understanding, political and patriotic organizations, and conservation and humane education groups, among many others. All are adult-sponsored, non-profit, and national in scope.

▶ *The Encyclopedia of Associations* (Gale Research, 1992). This directory of clubs, service groups, and organizations is updated several times a year. Region-al versions are now available which list several states in one volume.

▶ *Directories in Print, 1992* (Gale Research, 1992). A listing of all directories available—chamber of commerce directories, buyers' guides, career opportunities, transportation, Christmas decorations—you name it!

IMPORTANT
• • • • • • • • •

Before joining any club, group, or organization, check it out carefully. Make sure it represents your values and ideals. Get your parents involved in your decision.

136

Youth Clubs Providing Opportunities for Social Action

Boy Scouts of America
1325 Walnut Hill Lane
P.O. Box 152079
Irving, TX 75015-2079
(214) 580-2000
Contact for names and locations of local groups. Builds character, citizenship, and service.

Boys Clubs of America
771 First Ave.
New York, NY 10017
(212) 351-5900
Youth development and service.

Camp Fire, Inc.
4601 Madison Ave.
Kansas City, MO 64112-1278
(816) 756-1950
Serves girls and boys. Encourages self-reliance and good citizenship.

Co-Ette Club
2020 West Chicago Blvd.
Detroit, MI 48206
(313) 867-0880
Leadership training and community service for black high school girls.

4-H Youth Development
Cooperative Extension Service
U.S. Department of Agriculture
Washington, D.C. 20250
(202) 720-5853
Coeducational program for ages 8-19. Leadership development. Interest in nation's food and fiber agricultural systems and the family.

FFA (Future Farmers of America)
5632 Mt. Vernon Memorial Highway
P.O. Box 15160
Alexandria, VA 22309-0160
(703) 360-3600
Check with state or high school organizations for awards programs.

Girl Scouts of the U.S.A.
420 Fifth Ave.
New York, NY 10018
(212) 852-8000
Development of individual potential, values, and contributions to society.

Girls, Inc. (Girls Clubs of America)
30 East 33rd Street
New York, NY 10016
(212) 689-3700
Youth development and service. Serves girls ages 6-18.

National Association of Youth Clubs
5808 16th Street, N.W.
Washington, D.C. 20011
(202) 726-2044
Clubs for boys and girls 8-18, emphasizing character development and community service.

YMCA of the USA
101 N. Wacker Drive
Chicago, IL 60606
(312) 977-0031; (800) USA-YMCA
Youth programs which emphasize year-round development.

Environmental, Conservation, Humane (Animals), and Education Groups

Acid Rain Foundation
1410 Varsity Drive
Raleigh, NC 27606
(919) 828-9443
Educational Materials for K-12.

Adopt A Stream Foundation

P.O. Box 5558
Everett, WA 98201
(206) 388-3487
Guidelines for adopting a stream or wetland. Send a self-addressed, stamped envelope (SASE) and a small donation, if possible.

American Oceans Campaign

725 Arizona Ave.
Suite 102
Santa Monica, CA 90401
(310) 576-6162
or
235 Pennsylvania Ave., S.E.
Washington, D.C. 20003
(202) 544-3526
Information on protecting the ocean habitat.

American Society for the Prevention of Cruelty to Animals (ASPCA)

Education Department
424 East 92nd Street
New York, NY 10128
(212) 876-7700
Educational materials on humane treatment of animals.

Audubon Society

700 Broadway
New York, NY 10003
(212) 979-3000
Information on organizing youth groups in environmental education.

Caretakers of the Environment, International

2216 Schiller Ave.
Wilmette, IL 60091
Local winning high school projects attend international workshops around the world. Accommodations and food provided for participants.

Center for Clean Air Policy

444 North Capitol Street
Suite 602
Washington, D.C. 20001
(202) 624-7709
Publishes technical reports on clean air issues, including acid rain, global warming, and toxins.

C.A.P.E. (Children's Alliance for Protection of the Environment)

P.O. Box 307
Austin, TX 78767
(512) 476-2273
Linking children in environmental action projects.

Children's Rainforest

P.O. Box 936
Lewiston, ME 04240
Information on Children's Project to save the rain forest in Costa Rica.

Citizen's Clearinghouse for Hazardous Wastes

P.O. Box 6806
Falls Church, VA 22040
(703) 237-2249
Several handbooks and "how-to" information.

Cousteau Society

870 Greenbrier Circle
Suite 402
Chesapeake, VA 23320
Environmental education information.

Department of Commerce

Office of the Under Secretary
National Oceanic and Atmospheric Administration, Room 5128
Washington, D.C. 20230
Information about whales and dolphins.

Earth Kids

P.O. Box 3847
Salem, OR 97302
(503) 363-1896
Computer networking on the environment. No hook-up fee (Fidonet).

Earth Service Corps

909 Fourth Ave.
Seattle, WA 98104
(206) 382-5103
YMCA organization to encourage environmental action in youth.

Earth Train

99 Brookwood
Orinda, CA 94563
(510) 254-9101
Youth teaching youth in a cross-country environmental train and international projects.

Earthwatch

680 Mount Auburn Street, Box 403
Watertown, MA 02272
(617) 926-8200
Recruits volunteers for field research expeditions (archeology to zoology). Ages 16 and older. Operates in 36 countries and U.S.

EcoNet
18 DeBoom Street
San Francisco, CA 94107
(415) 442-0220
International computer-based communication
system for environmental preservation.

Friends of the Earth
1025 Vermont Ave., N.W.
Suite 300
Washington, D.C. 20005
(202) 783-7400

Global Re Leaf Program
American Forestry Association
P.O. Box 2000
Washington, D.C. 20013
(800) 368-5748, (202) 462-1177
Environmental education information.

Greenpeace
1436 U Street, N.W.
Washington, D.C. 20009
(202) 462-1177
Environmental education information.

Institute for Environmental Education
18554 Hoskins Road
Chagrin Falls, OH 44023
(216) 543-7303
Year-long environmental studies program.

Keep America Beautiful, Inc.
9 West Broad Street
Stamford, CT 06902
(203) 323-8987
Information on solid waste management and litter
prevention.

KAP (Kids Against Pollution)
P.O. Box 775
Closter, NJ 07624
(201) 784-0668
This is a kids' networking group against pollution.
Send $10.00 to join the network.

Kids F.A.C.E. (Kids for a Clean Environment)
P.O. Box 158254
Nashville, TN 37215
(615) 331-7381
Kids environmental action group. Sends out
newsletter.

K.S.E. (Kids for Saving Earth)
P.O. Box 47247
Plymouth, MN 55447-9764
Kids environmental action club. Sends out
newsletter.

Kids S.T.O.P.
P.O. Box 471
Forest Hills, NY 11375
Kids environmental action group. Send seven 29-
cent stamps for an action kit and membership
information.

Monteverde Conservation League
Apartado 10165
San Jose, Costa Rica
Information on environment, conservation, other
groups.

National Arbor Day Foundation
100 Arbor Ave.
Nebraska City, NE 68410
(402) 474-5655
Join organization and receive free seedlings. Also
information on trees.

**National Association for Humane and
Environmental Education**
67 Salem Road
East Haddam, CT 06423
(203) 434-8666
Information on *Kind News* newspaper.

**National Coalition Against the Misuse of
Pesticides**
701 E Street, S.E., Suite 200
Washington, D.C. 20003
(202) 543-5450
Information on alternatives to pesticides.

National Energy Information Center
EI-231, Energy Information Administration
Room 1F-048, Forrestal Bldg.
1000 Independence Ave., S.W.
Washington, D.C. 20585
(202) 586-8800
Information on Energy.

National Geographic Kids Network
1145 17th Street, N.W.
Washington, D.C. 20036
(202) 857-7000
A telecommunications-based science curriculum
which allows for sharing of environmental data.
Fourth through sixth grades.

National Solid Waste Management Association
1730 Rhode Island Ave., N.W.
Suite 1000
Washington, D.C. 20036
(202) 659-4613
Information on recycling and solid waste
management.

National Wildlife Federation
Correspondence Division
1400 16th Street, N.W.
Washington, D.C. 20036
(800) 432-6564, (703) 790-4000
Educational materials.

Natural Guard
142 Howard Ave.
New Haven, CT 06519
(203) 787-0229
Works with inner-city kids in community action.

Natural Resources Defense Council
Public Education Department
40 West 20th Street
New York, NY 10011
(212) 727-2700
Information on citizen education and action.

People for the Ethical Treatment of Animals
P.O. Box 42516
Washington, D.C. 20015
Information on fair treatment of animals.

Rainforest Alliance
270 Lafayette Street
Suite 512
New York, NY 10012
(212) 941-1900
Information on saving rainforests.

Sierra Club
730 Polk Street
San Francisco, CA 94109
(415) 776-2211
Environmental information. Ask about Inner City
    Outings, wilderness adventures.

Student Action Corps for Animals
P.O. Box 15588
Washington, D.C. 20003
(202) 543-8983
Seeks to empower high school students to work for
    animal rights movement.

Touch America Project
U.S. Forest Service
P.O. Box 96090
Washington, D.C. 20090
(703) 235-8855
Volunteer conservation program on public lands
    for ages 14-17.

Transportation Alternatives
P.O. Box 2087
New York, NY 10009
Environmentally aware ways to travel.

United Nations Environment Program (UNEP)
Liaison Office
DC1 Bldg.-590
1 U.N. Plaza
New York, NY 10017
(212) 963-4931
Information on Youth Environment Forum,
    environmental education.

**United Nations Environmental Youth
Ambassador—Canada**
Ms. Beatrice Olivastri, Executive Director
National Survival Institute
249 Nepean Street
Ottawa K2P 0B7, Canada
For environmental information and lists of
    countries around the world with youth
    organizations. Share your success stories.

U.S. Environmental Protection Agency
Office of Environmental Education
Coordinator of Youth Programs (A-107)
401 M Street, S.W.
Washington, D.C. 20460
(202) 260-8749
Environmental education materials for K-12, (202)
    260-7751; grant information, (202) 260-4484

U.S. Fish and Wildlife Service
Department of the Interior
18th and C Streets, N.W.
Washington, D.C. 20240
(202) 208-5634
Information on endangered species. Wetland
    information, (703) 358-1784.

Isaac Walton League
1401 Wilson Blvd., Level B
Arlington, VA 22209
(703) 528-1818
Information regarding protection of natural
    resources.

Washington State Department of Ecology
Litter Control and Recycling Program
4350 150th Ave., N.E.
Redmond, WA 98052
Educational materials for K-12.

World Wildlife Fund
1250 24th Street, N.W.
Washington, D.C. 20037
(202) 293-4800
Information on protection of endangered wildlife;
    wetlands; rain forests in Asia, Latin America,
    Africa.

Political Organizations

Constitutional Rights Foundation
1235 Jefferson Davis Highway
Arlington, VA 22202
A non-partisan educational foundation. It
promotes citizen involvement in government.

Frontlash
815 16th Street, N.W.
Washington, D.C. 20006
(202) 783-3993
High school and college students. Labor
movement and social progress. Support group
of the AFL-CIO.

**Girls State/Girls Nation—
Boys State/Boys Nation**
Contact your state American Legion Headquarters.
Youth citizenship training program which teaches
how American government functions.
Leadership training.

Junior Statesmen of America
Junior Statesmen Foundation
650 Bair Island Road, Suite 201
Redwood City, CA 94063
(800) 334-5353; (415) 366-2700
Prepares young leaders for participation in
democratic self-government.

**National Association for the Advancement
of Colored People (NAACP)**
Youth and College Division
4805 Mt. Hope Drive
Baltimore, MD 21215-3297
(410) 358-8900, Ext. 9142
Seeks equal rights and elimination of racial
prejudice.

National Teen Age Republican Headquarters
P.O. Box 1896
Manassas, VA 22110
(703) 368-4214
Principles of free enterprise, constitutional
government, patriotism. STARS groups for 9-12
year olds.

People's Anti War Mobilization
1470 Irving Street, N.W.
Washington, D.C. 20010
(202) 332-5041
High school and college students who oppose war,
imperialism, racism, discrimination.

Young Americans for Freedom
14018-A Sullyfield Circle
Chantilly, VA 22021
(703) 378-1178
Conservative political youth organization
promoting free enterprise, national defense, etc.
Ages 14-39.

Young Democrats of America
c/o Democratic National Committee
430 S. Capitol Street, S.E.
Washington, D.C. 20003
(202) 863-8000
Fosters aims of the Democratic Party for ages
18-30.

**Youth Section of the Democratic Socialists
of America**
15 Dutch Street, Suite 500
New York, NY 10038
(212) 962-0390
Youth to age 31. Protects and expands rights of
workers, women, minorities, all people.

Global, Peace, Space Groups

AFS International/Intercultural Programs
313 East 43rd Street
New York, NY 10017
(212) 949-4242
Promotes international exchange of high school
students in over 60 countries. May live with
host families. Volunteer work included.

**American Friends Service Committee Youth
Programs**
1501 Cherry Street
Philadelphia, PA 19102
(215) 241-7295
Offers work camps and service opportunities in
Mexico for ages 18-26.

Children of War
Religious Task Force
85 South Oxford Street
Brooklyn, NY 11217
(718) 858-6882
International peace leadership program for ages 13-18. Membership from 13 countries. Designed to counter racism and violence among youth.

Children's Campaign for Nuclear Disarmament
14 Everit Street
New Haven, CT 06511
(203) 226-3694
Completely youth-run organization. Ages 18 and younger. Dedicated to ending the arms race.

Council on International Education Exchange
205 East 42nd Street
New York, NY 10017
(212) 661-1414
Volunteer service programs at high school and college levels. Information on over 200 opportunities for study, adventures, worldwide travel for ages 12-18.

International Christian Youth Exchange
134 West 26th Street
New York, NY 10001
(212) 206-7307
International experiences for ages 16-35 in 32 countries. Volunteer work in the field.

International Pen Friends
Box 290065
Brooklyn, NY 11229-0001
Headquartered in Dublin, Ireland, this group can connect you with 250,000 pen pals of all ages in 153 countries. Send a self-addressed, stamped envelope (SASE) for information.

KIDLINK
4815 Saltrod
Norway
U.S. phone (203) 693-8544
Kids sharing information from around the world

Kids Meeting Kids
380 Riverside Drive
New York, NY 10025
(212) 662-2327
Organization of kids ages 5-19 from around the world which promotes peace, fair treatment of young people, and a better world. Send SASE for more information.

Model U.N. (United Nations)
U.N. Association of the U.S.A.
485 Fifth Ave.
New York, NY 10017-6104
(212) 697-3232
Opportunities for young people to participate in model United Nations and youth programs.

NASA Headquarters
Code XEP
Washington, D.C. 20546
Information on space and the space program.

Open Door Student Exchange
250 Fulton Ave.
P.O. Box 71
Hempstead, NY 11551
(516) 486-7330
International educational exchange organization. High school students and families. Scholarships available.

PEACENET
18 DeBoom Street
San Francisco, CA 94107
(415) 442-0220
International computer-based communication system for promotion of peace.

World Future Society
7910 Woodmont Ave., Suite 450
Bethesda, MD 20814
(301) 656-8274
Promotes study of the future. Draws from U.S. and 80 countries. Serves as clearinghouse for information about the future.

World Learning
Kipling Road, Box 676
Brattleboro, VT 05302
(802) 257-7751
Citizen exchange, language instruction, international development and training. Summer home stays for high school students and young adults.

World Vision
Public Relations Department
919 West Huntington Drive
Monrovia, CA 91016
(818) 357-7979
Offers development assistance for individuals and communities with aim to promote self-reliance.

Social Action, Community Development Groups, Health, Substance Abuse, Suicide, Teen Pregnancy Prevention, Etc.

Action
1100 Vermont Ave., N.W.
Washington, D.C. 20525
(800) 424-8867
Student Community Service Program, Volunteers in Service to America (VISTA), Foster Grandparent, Action Drug Alliance (which provides funding/seed money for local substance abuse education and prevention).

American Red Cross
Program and Services Department
Youth Associate
431 18th Street, N.W.
Washington, D.C. 20006
(202) 639-3039
Encourages volunteerism, leadership development, community involvement.

America's PRIDE Program
World Youth Against Drugs
National Parents' Resource Institute for Drug Education
50 Hurt Plaza, Suite 210
Atlanta, GA 30303
(404) 577-4500
Dedicated to creating drug-free youth.

Big Brothers/Big Sisters of America
230 North 13th Street
Philadelphia, PA 19107
(215) 567-7000
Adult volunteers aid youth in problems of drug abuse, teen pregnancy, foster care, juvenile delinquency, sexual abuse, etc.

Child Welfare League of America
440 First Street, N.W., Suite 310
Washington, D.C. 20001
(202) 638-2952
National network of youth programs focusing on youth as trainers for teen pregnancy prevention, quality parenting, self-sufficiency.

Childhelp USA
6463 Independence Ave.
Woodland Hills, CA 91367
(800) 4-A-CHILD
Child abuse prevention, information, counseling, contacts, hotline.

Close Up Foundation
44 Canal Center Plaza
Alexandria, VA 22314
(703) 706-3300
A program that gives kids a close-up look at how government works, teaching civic responsibility and social action. Also has educational materials.

Educators for Social Responsibility
23 Garden Street
Cambridge, MA 02138
(617) 492-1764
Information about how to involve your teachers in creating new ways of education for active and responsible participation in the world.

Guardian Angels
Junior Guardian Angels
982 East 89th Street
Brooklyn, NY 11236-3911
(718) 649-2607, (212) 397-7822
Trains volunteers to seek to deter crime through unarmed street patrols. Over 50 participating cities. Junior Angels for ages 11-15.

Habitat for Humanity, International
121 Habitat Street
Americus, GA 31709
(912) 924-6935
Deals with problems of the homeless and people with disabilities.

Just Say No Clubs
"Just Say No" Foundation
2101 Webster, Suite 1300
Oakland, CA 94612
(800) 258-2766, (510) 451-6666
   Prevention of drug use by children and teens.

National Clearinghouse for Alcohol and Drug Information
P.O. Box 2345
Rockville, MD 20847
(800) 729-6686, (301) 468-2600
A federal clearinghouse for information and
   educational materials for drug and alcohol
   abuse prevention.

National Collaboration for Youth
1319 F Street, N.W., Suite 601
Washington, D.C. 20004
(202) 347-2080
Consortium of 15 major voluntary youth-serving
   organizations. Advocates needs of youth in
   substance abuse, youth employment, juvenile
   justice, etc.

National Crime Prevention Council
1700 K Street, N.W., 2nd Floor
Washington, D.C. 20006
(202) 466-6272
Information on fighting crime.

National Network of Runaway and Youth Services, Inc.
1319 F Street, N.W., Suite 401
Washington, D.C. 20004
(202) 783-7949
Network of services for youth, including
   delinquency, drug use, adolescent pregnancy
   prevention, crisis intervention, independent
   living, family therapy, etc. Direction and
   training for youth.

National Self-Help Clearinghouse
25 West 43rd Street, Room 620
New York, NY 10036
(212) 642-2944
Provides information and referral to self-help
   groups throughout the country. How to
   organize your own groups.

NYLC (National Youth Leadership Council)
1910 West County Road B
Roseville, MN 55113
(612) 631-3672
Clearinghouse for Serve America. Offers
   information, projects, materials, training,
   technical assistance for service learning.

Natural Guard
142 Howard Ave.
New Haven, CT 06519
(203) 787-0229
Hands-on children's organization which assists
   youth in identifying and solving their own
   community problems.

Planned Parenthood Federation of America
810 Seventh Ave.
New York, NY 10019
(212) 541-7800
Information on teen pregnancy prevention.

Public Health Service
Public Affairs
Hubert H. Humphrey Bldg.
200 Independence Ave., S.W., Room 721-H
Washington, D.C. 20201
(202) 690-6867
Information on health issues.

Serve America (National Service Commission)
529 14th Street N.W., Suite 452
Washington, D.C. 20045
(202) 724-0600
Information on state directors for youth service,
   and service learning.

Special Olympics, International
1350 New York Ave., N.W., Suite 500
Washington, D.C. 20005
(202) 628-3630
Information on Special Olympics.

Students Against Drunk Driving (SADD)
P.O. Box 800
Marlboro, MA 01752
(508) 481-3568
Student organization to combat drunk driving.

Volunteers of America, Inc.
3939 North Causeway Blvd., Suite 400
Metairie, LA 70002
(504) 837-2652
Wide range of youth services and volunteer
   opportunities.

Youth Service America
1101 15th Street, N.W., Suite 200
Washington, D.C. 20005
(202) 296-2992
Promotes youth service programs and offers
   technical assistance.

AWARDS AND RECOGNITION FOR KIDS

Many national groups recognize kids who have made contributions in their communities. Some award you with certificates or trophies; other offer cash prizes or expenses-paid trips to receive the awards. Contact them by mail or phone to find out specifics. If you ask at your local youth, church, school groups, city and state agencies, you will probably discover additional award possibilities.

For more information on awards check your library reference desk for *Awards, Honors, and Prizes*, Vol. 1, U.S. and Canada (Gale Research, 1992).

America the Beautiful Fund
219 Shoreham Bldg.
Washington, D.C. 20005
(800) 522-3557, (202) 638-1649
Administrates "Operation Green Plant," a national recognition program for projects utilizing free seed packets.

American Health Care Association
Public Relations Office
1201 L Street, N.W.
Washington, D.C. 20005-4014
(202) 842-4444
Awards "Teen Volunteer of the Year" for volunteer work in nursing homes. Nominated by state health care associations. Awards plaque, gift, and expenses-paid trip to convention. August 15 deadline. Ages 13-19.

American Red Cross
National Office of Volunteers
Attention: Awards and Recognitions
17th and D Streets, N.W.
Washington, D.C. 20006
(202) 639-3035
Awards the "Woodrow Wilson Award" to a youth under 21 for contributions to the Red Cross and community. Nomination by chapters. December 15 deadline.

Boys and Girls Clubs of America
771 First Ave.
New York, NY 10017
(212) 351-5900
Awards the "National Youth of the Year Award" for contribution to home, school, church, community, and boys/girls clubs. Local, state, regional winners. National winners receive a $5,000 scholarship sponsored by *Reader's Digest*. Ages 12-18.

Chevron Conservation Awards Programs
P.O. Box 7753
San Francisco, CA 94120
(415) 894-2457
Annual awards of $1,000 to volunteer, organizations for conservation efforts. December deadline.

CLASS ACT Environmental Challenge
Amway/*Newsweek* Award
Creative Resources
220 Lyon Street, N.W., Suite 567
Grand Rapids, MI 49503-2210
(616) 456-1500
Awards for demonstrating outstanding projects to help preserve the environment. Cash awards to schools, gifts, write-up in *Newsweek*.

Colgate Youth of America Award

P.O. Box 1058, F.D.R. Station
New York, NY 10150-1058
(212) 736-0564

Open to Boy Scouts/Girl Scouts, Boys Clubs/Girls Clubs, Camp Fire, and 4-H Clubs. Forty-three prizes from $100 to $2,000. March deadline.

Congressional Award Foundation

6520 Georgetown Pike
McLean, VA 22101
(703) 761-6150

Recognizes youth for voluntary public service and personal excellence. Bronze, silver, gold medals. Ages 14-23. Gold medal (January deadline) awarded in Washington, D.C.

Freedoms Foundation at Valley Forge

Route 23
Valley Forge, PA 19481
(215) 933-8825

National awards for schools, individuals, organizations for promoting responsible citizenship.

Future Farmers of America (FFA)

5632 Mt. Vernon Memorial Highway
P.O. Box 15160
Alexandria, VA 22309-0160
(703) 360-3600

Recognitions through high school chapters for community service, safety activities, agriculture awards, etc.

Future Problem Solving Program (FPSP)

315 West Huron Street, Suite 140B
Ann Arbor, MI 48103-4203
(313) 998-7FPS (7377)

Sponsors an annual awards competition for Community Problem Solving/Future Problem Solving for those registered in FPSP. Individual state deadlines for FSP. Winners go to national competition. March 31 deadline, Community Problem Solving national competition.

The Giraffe Project

P.O Box 759
Langley, WA 98260
(206) 221-7989

Recognizes courage of individuals of all ages who "stick their necks out" for others. May deadline. Also offers training in community action.

Girl Scouts/Boy Scouts/4-H Clubs, etc.

Check local chapters for awards and recognitions.

International Juvenile Officers' Association

309 Spring Hill Road
Monroe, CT 06468
(516) 747-2948

Gives "Joseph G. Phelan Award" to honor a youth for outstanding service in delinquency prevention and control. May deadline.

International Society of Crime Prevention Practitioners

1696 Connor Drive
Pittsburgh, PA 15129-9035
(412) 655-1600

Awards to crime prevention programs at national Explorers' Conference. Alternate years.

Jefferson Awards

American Institute for Public Service
621 Delaware Street, Suite 300
Newcastle, DE 19720
(302) 323-9659

Sponsored by *Weekly Reader* for outstanding public service. Annual awards. State winners receive Jefferson Award, medal, and expenses-paid trip (with chaperon) to Washington, D.C. February 16 deadline.

Joint Action in Community Service

5225 Wisconsin Ave., Suite 404
Washington, D.C. 20015
(202) 537-0996

Awards for volunteer work in community.

Junior Civitan International

Leadership Development Department
P.O. Box 130744
Birmingham, AL 35213-0744
(205) 591-8910

Awards to outstanding total youth and youth project for all areas of youth work, community service, and projects on behalf of people who are physically and mentally challenged. Open to club members. Plaque awarded.

Keep America Beautiful, Inc.

Awards Program Coordinator
9 West Broad Street
Stamford, CT 06902
(203) 323-8987

Annual awards to youth and school groups for environmental improvement, etc. August 18 deadline. Presentation of awards in Washington, D.C.

Kids Care

Scholastic News, Inc.
555 Broadway
New York, NY 10012
Awards class $1,000 for favorite charity; awards
school $5,000 for favorite charity.

National Advisory Council on Indian Education

Switzer Bldg., Room 4072
330 C Street, S.W.
Washington, D.C. 20202
(202) 205-8353
Information on awards, scholarships, financial aid
for Native Americans.

National Arbor Day Foundation

Awards Committee
211 North 12th Street, Suite 501
Lincoln, NE 68508
(402) 474-5655
Offers awards to individuals and schools for work
in tree planing, stewardship, or education.

National Association for the Advancement of Colored People (NAACP)

Check local branches for awards and recognitions.

National Association of Professional Insurance Agents

400 North Washington Street
Alexandria, VA 22314
(703) 836-9340
Awards "Alert Youth Award" for heroism in saving
life or property. Ages 18 and younger.

National Safety Council

Community Safety Programs Area
1121 Spring Lake Drive
Itasca, IL 60143-3201
(708) 285-1121
Recognizes accident prevention and promotion of
safety by youth groups and individuals.

National Wildlife Federation

National Conservation Awards Program
1400 16th Street, N.W.
Washington, D.C. 20036-2266
(202) 797-6800
Annual awards for contributions to the
environment. Awards statuette of whopping
crane and expenses-paid trip to receive award.

Parents Without Partners

Volunteer Services
8807 Colesville Road
Silver Spring, MD 20910
(301) 588-9354
Awards "Youth of the Year Award" to children of
members of organization for family, school,
community involvement.

J.C. Penney—"Golden Rule Awards"

P.O. Box 10001
Dallas, TX 75301
(214) 431-1000
Presents a "National Youth Award" for volunteer
service in community. Local award winner
receive bronze sculpture; the agency associated
with youth receives $1,000. The national award
is a bronze medallion, and the agency receives
$5,000; you receives $5,000 scholarship. Ages 18
and under.

President's Environmental Youth Awards

Coordinator for Youth Programs A-107
401 M Street, S.W.
Washington, D.C. 20460
(202) 260-8749
Ten regional winners and sponsor receive
expenses-paid trip to Washington, D.C., to
receive annual awards for contributions to
environment. Corporate sponsorships and
grants to winners.

The President's Volunteer Action Awards

Points of Light Foundation
1735 H Street, N.W.
Washington, D.C. 20006
(202) 223-9186
Annual awards for volunteer action presented by
the President at the White House in
Washington, D.C.

Religious Heritage of America

1750 South Brentwood Blvd.
St. Louis, MO 63144-1315
(314) 962-0001
Youth awards for service, leadership in church,
school, community. Awarded in October with
airfare and expenses for RHA weekend
conference.

United Nations Environment Program
Information and Public Affairs
P.O. Box 30552
Nairobi, Kenya
 Tel. 333930, Telex 22068,
 Cable address UNITERRA NAIROBI
 Recognizes environmental contributions by
youth for Global 500 Awards.

U.S. Department of Justice Programs
Young American Medals Committee
10th and Constitution Ave., N.W.
Washington, D.C. 20001
(202) 307-0781
Awards "Young American Medal for Bravery" and
 "Young American Medal for Service." For
 outstanding character and community service.
 Ages 18 and under. Nominations must come
 from state governors. Awards expenses-paid
 trip to Washington, D.C., to receive medal.

Windstar Youth Award
2317 Snowmass Creed Road
Snowmass, CO 81654
(303) 927-4777
Annual scholarship award for youth who shows
 leadership in environmental action.

Yoshiyama Award
P.O. Box 19247
Washington, D.C. 20036
(202) 457-0588
Awards $5,000 to 6-8 high school seniors for
 extraordinary community service.

BOOKS

Check your library for these and other books about government, the environment, social action, and other subjects.

Books for Young Readers about Government, Citizenship, and Rights

American Freedom and The Bill of Rights by William Wise (Parents Magazine Press, 1975). Very easy to read.

The Bill of Rights and Landmark Cases by Edmund Lindop (Franklin Watts, 1989). Discusses landmark cases dealing with the Bill of Rights (Constitutional Law Amendments 1-10).

Censorship in the U.S., edited by Grant S. McClellan (H.W. Wilson, 1967). History of censorship, Supreme Court, politics, education, thinking.

A Children's Chorus: Celebrating the 30th Anniversary of the Universal Declaration of the Rights of the Child by UNICEF (E.P. Dutton, 1989). Declaration of the Rights of the Child. Illustrations and principles.

Civics for Democracy: Ralph Nader Presents by Katherine Isaac (The Center for Study of Responsive Law and Essential Information, 1992). History of citizen movements and action-oriented guide to participation.

Civics: Citizens and Society by Allan Knownslar and Terry L. Smart (McGraw-Hill, 1983). Role of citizens.

Civil Rights: The Challenge of the 14th Amendment by Peter Goldman (Coward McCann, 1965). History of the black movement for equal rights.

The First Freedom: The Tumultuous History of Free Speech in America by Nat Hentoff (Delacorte, 1988). History of free speech.

Freedom by Wilma Pitchford Hays (Coward McCann, 1958). History of important U.S. events.

Freedom: The Story of Your Rights as an American by Earl Schenck Miers (Grosset and Dunlop, 1965). Story of liberty and freedom in U.S.

Freedom of Religion by J. Edward Evans, American Politics series (Lerner Pub. Co., 1990). Surveys the history of freedom of religion in the U.S. and the court cases that defined it.

The Freedom of Speech in America by Ravina Gelfand (Lerner, 1968). History of free speech.

How We Choose a President by Lee Learner Gray (St. Martin's Press, 1972). Describes Presidential elections.

Human Rights by Gerald S. Snyder (Franklin Watts, 1980). Discusses human rights, freedom of expression, racial discrimination, religious freedom, women's rights, rights of children and the disabled.

Issues in American History: The Right to Vote by Carole Lynn Corbin (Franklin Watts, 1985). The history of voting rights for blacks, women, young voters.

Justice by Kevin Osborn, The Values Library series (Rosen Pub. Group, Inc., 1992). Discusses the meaning of justice. Gives examples of "just" behavior and its importance in life.

A Matter of Principle by Susan B. Pfeffer (Delacorte, 1982). A fictional account of a high school underground newspaper that conflicts with a principal's ideas.

Opposing Viewpoints series (Greenhaven Press, 1992). Both sides of issues and controversies on dozens of subjects. Great for debates.

The Pizza Problem: Democracy in Action by Maryrose Eannace (Policy Studies Associates, 1990). A practical case of democracy in action in a high school.

Politics by Patricia Maloney Markun (Franklin Watts, 1970). What politics means; how people get what they want through politics; how politics has changed; future politics.

Responsibility by Glenn A. Cheney (Franklin Watts, 1985). Describes the responsibilities of citizenship.

Separation of Church and State by Irene Cumming Kleeberg (Franklin Watts, 1983). The history of keeping government and religion separate.

Taking On the Press: Constitutional Rights in Conflict by Melvyn B. Zerman (Harper Junior Books, 1986). Historical accounts of conflicts between the press and rights of individuals.

Think About Our Rights: Civil Liberties and the U.S. by Reginald Wilson (Walker and Company, 1988). Describes the civil rights movements for minorities, women, youth, and future outlook.

The Unions: What They Are, How They Came to Be, How They Affect Each of Us by Alvin Schwartz (Viking Press, 1972). History of the labor movement and unions.

Books about the Environment

Can the Whale Be Saved? Questions about the Natural World and the Threat to Its Survival by Dr. Philip Whitfield and the Natural History Museum (Viking Kestral, 1989). Short answers to over 100 questions about our environment. For young readers.

Caring for Trees on City Streets by Joan Edwards for The Environmental Action Coalition (Charles Scribner's Sons, 1976). How to care for trees.

The Earth Report: The Essential Guide to Global Ecological Issues, edited by Edward Goldsmith and Nicolas Hildyard (Price Stern Sloan, 1988). Six essays and hundreds of shorter articles about the environment.

Ecology by Susan Diffenderfer (Zephyr Press, 1984). Hands-on activities for self-directed learning for kids.

50 Simple Things Kids Can Do To Save the Earth by John Javna and The Earthworks Group (Andrews and McMeel, 1990). Facts, experiments, and exciting things to do.

The Green Consumer by John Elkington, Julia Hailes, and Joel Makower (Penguin Books, 1990). Information about buying products that don't hurt the earth.

The Green Lifestyle Handbook: 1001 Ways You Can Heal the Earth by Jeremy Rifkin (Henry Holt and Company, 1990). How to live in a responsible way; "cruelty-free" products; state recycling phone numbers.

Kids Can Save the Animals! by Ingrid Newkirk (Warner, 1990). Facts about animals and animal-friendly companies, and things kids can do to help save animals.

Kids for Saving the Earth Guidebook. Tells how to join this kids' organization or start your own KSE neighborhood club; gives environmental information and activities. To order a FREE copy, write: Target, P.O. Box 47247, Plymouth, MN 55447-0247.

The State of the States by Scott Ridley (1987). Compares states on environmental programs—air, soil, solid and hazardous wastes, groundwater, energy. To order a FREE copy, write: Fund for Renewable Energy and the Environment, 1001 Connecticut Ave. N.W, Suite 638, Washington, D.C. 20006.

Our Only Earth series by Mikki McKisson and Linda McRae Campbell (Zephyr Press, 1990). A series of books on rain forests, pollution, poverty, war, oceans, endangered species, with information and activities for young readers.

Books on Creative Thinking and Problem-Solving

Be a Problem Solver by Bob Stanish and Bob Eberle (DOK Publishers, 1984). Applications for CPS For Kids (described below). Identifies problems for kids to do in independent study.

Creative Problem Solving for Teens by Patricia A. Elwell (DOK Publishers, 1990). All kinds of problem solving; written for teens.

CPS For Kids by Bob Stanish and Bob Eberle (DOK Publishers, 1989). A book on creative problem solving.

From Basics to Breakthroughs by Roger Firestien (DOK Publishers, 1989). How to identify a problem and put solutions into action.

Futuristics by Joey Tanner (Zephyr Press, 1981). Analyzing trends, making predictions, and planning creatively for the future.

Visionizing by Sydney Parnes (DOK Publishers, 1988). Putting dreams for the future into reality.

TOOLS

BRAINSTORMING I: COME UP WITH IDEAS

IDEA — IDEAS

THAT MAKES ME THINK OF:

MORE WILD & CRAZY IDEAS — KEEP GOING:

BRAINSTORMING II: CHOOSE YOUR MAIN IDEA

AT THIS POINT, YOU HAVE MANY IDEAS, SOME OF THEM CRAZY. NOW YOU SHOULD CHOOSE AN IDEA TO WORK ON.

A. Ask yourself questions like: (1) Which idea might benefit the most people? (2) Which idea might have the best chance to succeed? (3) Which idea might cost the least to do? (4) Which idea might make the biggest difference? (5) Which idea do I like the best?

Think of questions which will help you make a good choice.

QUESTIONS

1. _____

2. _____

3. _____

4. _____

5. _____

B. Choose one basic idea to work with: _____

C. Now list the steps to carry out your Plan of Action. Examples: Give speeches at the Community Council; write letters to the mayor; write a news release for TV and radio.

Then write down who will be responsible for each step, and when.

PLAN OF ACTION

ACTIVITY	WHO DOES IT?	WHEN?
1.		
2.		
3.		
4.		
5.		
6.		
7.		

(Use another sheet of paper if you need more space)

PHONE FORM

"Hello. May I please speak to _____ **or someone in public relations or public information?"**
CONTACT'S NAME

"My name is _____ **and I'm from** _____**."**
YOUR NAME   YOUR SCHOOL/GRADE/ORGANIZATION

1. PURPOSE (what you're going to say or ask): _____

_____

_____

_____

_____

2. INFORMATION (write down what your contact tells you): _____

_____

_____

_____

_____

(Attach more paper if you need it.)

"Thank you very much."

_____   _____
YOUR NAME   DATE OF CALL

_____
SCHOOL/GROUP PHONE

                                              _____
                                              SCHOOL/GROUP ADDRESS

_____   _____
CONTACT'S NAME   TITLE

_____
CONTACT'S PHONE

                                              _____
                                              CONTACT'S ADDRESS

LETTER FORM

Your Name
The Name of Your School or Group
Your Home, School, or Group Street Address
City, State, ZIP

Date

Name of Person You Are Writing To
Title of Person You Are Writing To
Name of Newspaper, Office, or Company
Street Address
City, State, ZIP

(Name of Person You Are Writing To):

(INDENT THE BEGINNING OF EACH PARAGRAPH, IF YOU WISH.)

_____

_____

_____

_____

_____

_____

_____

_____

_____

Sincerely,

Your Name
Your Grade

INTERVIEW FORM

In Person _____
By Phone _____
By Letter _____

_____
NAME OF PERSON INTERVIEWED

_____
PHONE NUMBER

_____
DATE OF INTERVIEW

_____
TITLE

_____
COMPANY/ORGANIZATION NAME

_____
STREET ADDRESS

_____
CITY, STATE, ZIP

From: _____ To: _____
TIME

QUESTIONS/ANSWERS

_____

_____

_____

_____

_____

_____

_____

_____

(Attach more paper if you need it.)

_____
YOUR NAME

_____
YOUR SCHOOL/GRADE/ORGANIZATION

SURVEY FORM

This survey form is for one person's responses to many questions.

Write your questions on the longer lines. Write responses (SA = Strongly Agree, A = Agree, D = Disagree, SD = Strongly Disagree) on the shorter lines to the left of the question numbers.

____ 1. _____

_____

____ 2. _____

_____

____ 3. _____

_____

____ 4. _____

_____

____ 5. _____

_____

____ 6. _____

_____

____ 7. _____

_____

____ 8. _____

_____

____ 9. _____

_____

____ 10. _____

_____

SURVEY FORM

This survey form can be used for many people's responses to the same questions.

QUESTIONS

____ 1. _____
_____

____ 2. _____
_____

____ 3. _____
_____

____ 4. _____
_____

____ 5. _____
_____

RESPONSES

SA-STRONGLY AGREE   A-AGREE   D-DISAGREE   SD-STRONGLY DISAGREE

	SA	A	D	SD	UNDECIDED
1.	*				
2.					
3.					
4.					
5.					

* Mark a line for each response (⫴⊬).

TABULATION OF SURVEY RESULTS

	SA	A	D	SD	UNDECIDED
1.	*				
2.					
3.					
4.					
5.					
6.					
7.					
8.					
9.					
10.					

SA-STRONGLY AGREE   A-AGREE   D-DISAGREE   SD-STRONGLY DISAGREE

* Write the number of people who strongly agree with question #1.

COMMENTS: _____

_____

_____

_____

_____

_____

PETITION

_____
(TITLE OF PETITION)

A Petition of: _____

Addressed to: _____

WE THE UNDERSIGNED WOULD LIKE TO BRING YOUR ATTENTION TO THE FOLLOWING PROBLEM, WITH RECOMMENDATION(S):

_____

_____

_____

_____

AGREED UPON BY THE FOLLOWING PEOPLE:

	Name	Address/Group/School	Phone
1.	_____	_____	_____
2.	_____	_____	_____
3.	_____	_____	_____
4.	_____	_____	_____
5.	_____	_____	_____
6.	_____	_____	_____
7.	_____	_____	_____
8.	_____	_____	_____
9.	_____	_____	_____
10.	_____	_____	_____
11.	_____	_____	_____
12.	_____	_____	_____
13.	_____	_____	_____
14.	_____	_____	_____
15.	_____	_____	_____

PROPOSAL

_____
(TITLE OF PROPOSAL)

Presented to: _____

Presented by: _____

Date: _____ School/Organization: _____

DESCRIPTION OF PROPOSAL:

_____

_____

_____

ORGANIZATIONAL PLAN:

_____

_____

_____

NEEDS:

_____

_____

_____

BUDGET:

_____

_____

_____

TIME LINE:

_____

_____

_____

GRANT APPLICATION CHECKLIST

Most grant applications ask you to provide the following information (some ask for even more). Check off each item as you complete it.

_____ **1.** Write a statement that explains your problem. Include strong facts and/or a story to support your statement.

_____ **2.** Describe your goals. Tell how your project will help to solve your problem. How will it improve on what has already been done by others?

_____ **3.** Describe your project.

_____ **4.** Tell how long you think your project will take.

_____ **5.** Tell how you plan to achieve your goals. Describe your method or list the steps you will take.

_____ **6.** Include a budget (how much money you will need, and how you plan to spend it). Include a list of what you think your expenses might be. Include any donations of time and materials you hope to receive.

_____ **7.** Tell how you plan to evaluate your progress—how you will show that you are achieving your goals.

_____ **8.** Include a statement of how your project might benefit the grantors (the organization or foundation you are asking to give you a grant). They like compliments as much as you do. For example, is there any way you can advertise that they funded your project?

_____ **9.** If you really want to get fancy, you might try using charts, graphs, videos, slides, audio tapes, or other creative ideas to make your grant stand out from the rest. How about a splash of color?

_____ **10.** Make and keep a copy of your grant application, in case the grantors lose the original. (It happens.)

_____ **11.** Send your application by registered mail. You will get a receipt saying that it has been received. Or, if possible, hand-carry it into the grantors' office.

_____ **12.** Follow up your application with letters, phone calls, or personal visits. Politely bug the grantors. This will let them know that you're serious about your request.

_____ **13.** If you receive your grant, be sure to send thank-you notes to your grantors (and anyone else who helped you to win your grant).

_____ **14.** You will probably be required to write a follow-up report. If you are, be sure to do it!

_____ **15.** If you don't receive your grant, request an evaluation from the grantors explaining their reasons for refusing your application. You'll learn important pointers you can use in future grant applications.

News Release

CONTACT:

FOR IMMEDIATE RELEASE

_____
NAME

_____
ADDRESS

_____
CITY, STATE, ZIP

_____
DATE

_____
PHONE

WHAT _____
_____
_____

WHO _____
_____
_____

WHEN _____
_____
_____

WHERE _____
_____
_____

DETAILS _____
_____
_____

PUBLIC SERVICE ANNOUNCEMENT (PSA)

_____
NAME OF YOUR GROUP

_____
ADDRESS

_____
TARGET AUDIENCE

_____   _____
BEGINNING DATE   ENDING DATE

_____
CONTACT PERSON

_____
PHONE

_____
(TOPIC)

TEXT

_____   _____
NUMBER OF
SECONDS   _____

                 _____

                 _____

_____   _____
NUMBER OF
WORDS   _____

                 _____

                 _____

                 _____

                 _____

END

PROCLAMATION

WHEREAS, _____
_____
_____
_____, and

WHEREAS, _____
_____
_____
_____, and

WHEREAS, _____
_____
_____
_____.

NOW, THEREFORE, _____
_____
_____
_____.

SIGNED THIS _____ DAY OF _____.

_____   _____

_____   _____

_____   _____

_____   _____

1. "Hello, my name is _____, and

I'm from _____ School/Troop/Organization.

I am supporting candidate or issue _____."

2. "Would you please tell me if you are registered to vote?"

☐ YES, registered

☐ NO, not registered

_____
(NAME)

_____
(ADDRESS OF HOUSE OR APARTMENT)

If the answer is YES, leave literature and thank the person.

If the answer is NO, do one of the following:

_____ (a) Register the resident in the Registration Book, or

_____ (b) Leave Mail-In Registration Form, or

_____ (c) Inform the resident of neighborhood registration.

_____
DATE(S)

_____
LOCATION(S)

_____

_____
PHONE NUMBER OF LOCAL REGISTRATION OFFICE

3. Thank the resident, and once again ask for support for your candidate or issue.

4. Comments from residents, or additional information:

_____

_____

_____

_____

Excuse me, please. May I talk with you for a moment?

My name is _____, and I'm representing kids from

_____ School (or group).

1. Would you please vote for/against _____?

<small>NUMBER & NAME OF BILL</small>

2. This is important because (give your "needs" statement—your reasons for supporting or opposing the bill) _____

_____

_____

3. Our solution is (tell how supporting or opposing the bill would help your cause) _____

_____

_____

4. Do you have any questions or suggestions? (write down any questions or suggestions the legislator has) _____

_____

_____

5. May I please have your support? ☐ YES ☐ NO ☐ MAYBE

6. Thank you very much for your time.

_____   _____
LEGISLATOR'S NAME

_____   _____   _____
YOUR NAME   GROUP   DATE

_____   _____
PHONE (GROUP)   ADDRESS (SCHOOL/GROUP/HOMETOWN)

_____
YOUR LEGISLATIVE DISTRICT

NAMES OF YOUR LEGISLATORS

LOBBYING BY PHONE

Hello. May I please speak to _____ or a legislative assistant?
LEGISLATOR'S NAME

My name is _____, and I'm from _____

_____School (or group).

1. Would you please vote for/against _____?
NUMBER & NAME OF BILL

2. **This is important because** (give your "needs" statement—your reasons for supporting or opposing the bill) _____

_____

3. **Our solution is** (tell how supporting or opposing the bill would help your cause) _____

_____

4. **Do you have any questions or suggestions?** (write down any questions or suggestions the legislator has) _____

_____

5. **May I please have your support?** ☐ YES   ☐ NO   ☐ MAYBE

6. **Thank you very much for your time.**

If the legislator isn't there, leave this message with the secretary: your name, school or group, phone number, school or group address, hometown, title and number of proposed bill, and how you want the legislator to vote.

_____   _____
LEGISLATOR'S NAME   TITLE

_____   _____
LEGISLATOR'S PHONE   ADDRESS

_____
WHICH COMMITTEES HAS THE LEGISLATOR SERVED ON?

_____   _____   _____
YOUR NAME   GROUP   DATE

_____   _____
PHONE (GROUP)   ADDRESS (SCHOOL/GROUP/HOMETOWN)

_____
YOUR LEGISLATIVE DISTRICT

_____
NAMES OF YOUR LEGISLATORS

LOBBYING BY TESTIFYING

My name is _____, and I'm from _____

_____School (or group). I/We would like to thank you for this opportunity.

I/We would also like to thank our sponsor, _____,
                                            NAME OF SPONSOR
for giving us valuable help.

I/We would like to encourage you to support/oppose:

_____
NUMBER & NAME OF BILL OR MEASURE

This is important because (give your "needs" statement—your reasons for supporting or opposing
the bill) _____

_____

_____

I/We believe the best solution is (tell how supporting or opposing the bill would help your cause)

_____

_____

(Tell how you have worked with your opposition):

_____

_____

(Tell who supports your position):

_____

_____

Do you have any questions or suggestions? _____

_____

_____

Thank you for your time. I/We would like to ask you for your support.

RESOLUTION

1. WHEREAS,   The _____

_____

_____

_____, and

2. WHEREAS,   The _____

_____

_____

_____, and

3. WHEREAS,   The _____

_____

_____

_____, therefore be it

4. RESOLVED,   That _____

_____

_____

_____, and be it further

5. RESOLVED,   That _____

_____

_____

_____, and be it finally

6. RESOLVED,   That _____

_____

_____

_____.

BIBLIOGRAPHY

Books

The Book of the States, 1988-89, Vol. 27, The Council of State Governments, Lexington, KY.

Broadcasting/Cable Yearbook, Washington, D.C., 1990.

A Citizen's Guide to Community Education on Global Issues, Sherry Rockey and Alice L. Hughey, Washington, D.C.: League of Women Voters Education Fund, 1988.

Civic Writing in the Classroom, Sandra Stotsky, Bloomington, IN: ERIC Clearinghouse for Social Studies/Social Science Education, 1987.

The Congressional Record, Washington, D.C.: U.S. Government Printing Office, printed daily; April 27, 1989, E 1407; May 27, 1988, S 7129.

The Constitution of the United States, various editions.

Creative Action Book, Sydney Parnes and Alex Osbourne, New York: Scribners, 1962.

Democracy at Work: A Study of Utah's Election Laws and Procedures, for the League of Women Voters, Bountiful, UT: Carr Printing Company, 1985.

Directory of American Youth Organizations: A Guide to Over 400 Clubs, Groups, Troops, Teams, Societies, Lodges, and More for Young People, Judith B. Erickson, Minneapolis, MN: Free Spirit Publishing Inc., 1990-91 edition.

How Our Laws Are Made, Washington, D.C.: U.S. Government Printing Office, Doc. No. 99-158, 1986.

If You Want Air Time: A Publicity Handbook, Jane Freundel Levey, Washington, D.C.: National Association of Broadcasters, 1987.

Making an Issue of It: The Campaign Handbook, Washington, D.C.: League of Women Voters, 1976.

The Municipal Year Book, Washington, D.C.: International City Management Association, 1989.

A Sourcebook for Creative Thinking, Sydney Parnes and Alex Osbourne, New York: Scribners, 1962.

The State of the States, Scott Ridley, Washington, D.C.: Fund for Renewable Energy and the Environment, 1987.

Tell It To Washington: A Guide for Citizen Action, Washington, D.C.: League of Women Voters Education Fund, Pub. No. 349, 1987-88.

U.S. Government Manual 89/90, Washington, D.C.: U.S. Government Printing Office, 1989-90.

Articles

Anne B. Crabbe, "The Future Problem Solving Program," *Educational Leadership*, September 1989, pp. 27-29.

John Dewey, "Experience and Thinking," *Democracy and Education*, New York: Macmillan, 1916 (paperback, 1966).

Virginia Goodale and Barbara A. Lewis, "Teaching the Skills of Democracy," *Instructor*, March 1973, pp. 70-76.

Barbara A. Lewis, "The Children's Cleanup Crusade," *Sierra*, March/April 1989, pp. 62-66.
—"Cleanup Crusade: Citizenship in Action," *Social Education*, April/May 1990, pp. 238-240.
—"Small Fry Community Activists," *The Civic Perspective*, Harvard Graduate School of Education, Summer/Fall 1988; pp. 6-8.

John O. McNeil, "The Social Reconstructionist Curriculum," *Curriculum: A Comprehensive Introduction*, Boston, MA: Little Brown, 1985, 3rd Edition. Now published by Harper Collins Publishers, Inc., Chicago, IL., 1990, 4th Edition.

Walt McPhie, "Dissenters in Democracy: Patriots or Subversives?" *The Social Studies*, Sept./Oct., 1986, Vol. 77, No. 5; Heldref Publications, Washington, D.C.

Joseph S. Renzulli, "Inservice Training for the Enrichment Trial Model," 1988.

Nancy Shute, "The Cleanup Crew," *Special Reports*, February-April 1990, pp. 46-52.

Stanley Smith, "Social Reconstruction as a Basic Curriculum Theory," *Fundamentals of Curriculum Development*, World Book, Chicago, IL: Scott Fetzer Co., 1989.

Jim Waltermire, "The Initiative Process, A Lesson in Citizen Participation for Montana Students," Montana; Montana State Capitol, 1984.

"The New Volunteers," *Newsweek*, Special Report, July 10, 1989, pp. 36-66.

"State Government," *World Book*, Chicago, IL: Scott Fetzer Company, 1987.

"Study Guide for 'How To,'" Salt Lake City, UT: The Utah Association of Women Executive Board, Salt Lake City, UT: 1985.

INDEX

ABOUT THE AUTHOR

Barbara Lewis has won over 25 awards and recognitions for excellence in writing and teaching and for her students' projects. She and her kids have been featured in many national magazines and newspapers, *The Congressional Record*, and on national and international television.

Barbara has lived in Indiana, New Jersey, Switzerland, Belgium, and Utah, where she was born and now resides. Besides teaching at Jackson Elementary in Salt Lake City, she has four children of her own and a wonderful husband.

One of Barbara's lifelong goals is to take time to explore the cavernous sewers of Paris, the scene of much drama in fiction and real life.

MORE FREE SPIRIT BOOKS

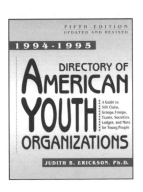

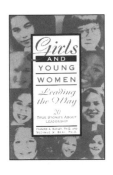